• CLASSIC AMERICAN FURNITURE SERIES •

AUTHENTIC SHAKER FURNITURE

KERRY PIERCE

POPULAR WOODWORKING BOOKS
CINCINNATI, OHIO
www.popularwoodworking.com

READ THIS IMPORTANT SAFETY NOTICE

To prevent accidents, keep safety in mind while you work. Use the safety guards installed on power equipment; they are for your protection. When working on power equipment, keep fingers away from saw blades, wear safety goggles to prevent injuries from flying wood chips and sawdust, wear earplugs to protect your hearing, and consider installing a dust vacuum to reduce the amount of airborne sawdust in your wood-shop. Don't wear loose clothing, such as neckties or shirts with loose sleeves, or jewelry, such as rings, necklaces or bracelets, when working on power equipment. Tie back long hair to prevent it from getting caught in your equipment. People who are sensitive to certain chemicals should check the chemical content of any product be-fore using it. The authors and editors who com-piled this book have tried to make the contents as accurate and correct as possible. Plans, illus-trations, photographs and text have been careful-ly checked. All instructions, plans and projects should be carefully read, studied and understood before beginning construction. In some photos, power tool guards have been removed to more clearly show the operation being demonstrated. Always use all safety guards and attachments that come with your power tools. Due to the variability of local conditions, construction mate-rials, skill levels, etc., neither the author nor Popular Woodworking Books assumes any re-sponsibility for any accidents, injuries, damages or other losses incurred resulting from the mate-rial presented in this book. Prices listed for supplies and equipment were current at the time of publication and are subject to change. Glass shelving should have all edges polished and must be tempered. Untempered glass shelves may shatter and can cause serious bodily injury. Tempered shelves are very strong and if they break will just crumble, minimizing person-al injury.

METRIC CONVERSION CHART

to convert	to	multiply by
Inches	Centimeters	2.54
Centimeters	Inches	0.4
Feet	Centimeters	30.5
Centimeters	Feet	0.03
Yards	Meters	0.9
Meters	Yards	1.1
Sq. Inches	Sq. Centimeters	6.45
Sq. Centimeters	Sq. Inches	0.16
Sq. Feet	Sq. Meters	0.09
Sq. Meters	Sq. Feet	10.8
Sq. Yards	Sq. Meters	0.8
Sq. Meters	Sq. Yards	1.2
Pounds	Kilograms	0.45
Kilograms	Pounds	2.2
Ounces	Grams	28.4
Grams	Ounces	0.035

Authentic Shaker Furniture. Copyright© 2004 by Kerry Pierce. Man-ufactured in China. All rights reserved. No part of this book may be re-produced in any form or by any electronic or mechanical means, including information storage and retrieval systems, without permission in writing from the publisher, except by a reviewer, who may quote brief passages in a review. Published by Popular Woodworking Books, an im-print of F&W Publications, Inc., 4700 East Galbraith Road, Cincinnati, Ohio, 45236. 800-289-0963. First edition.

Visit our Web site at www.popularwoodworking.com for information on more resources for woodworkers.

Other fine Popular Woodworking Books are available from your local bookstore or direct from the publisher.

08   07   06   05   04   5   4   3   2   1

Library of Congress Cataloging-in-Publication Data

Pierce, Kerry.
    Authentic Shaker furniture / by Kerry Pierce.-- 1st ed.
        p. cm. -- (Classic American furniture series)
    Includes index.
    ISBN 1-55870-657-7 (alk. paper)
    1. Furniture making. 2. Shaker furniture. I. Title. II. Series.

TT194.P517 2003
684.1'04--dc21
2003054946

ACQUISITIONS EDITOR: Jim Stack
EDITED BY: Jennifer Ziegler
DESIGNED BY: Brian Roeth
PRODUCTION COORDINATED BY: Mark Griffin and Robin Ritchie
LAYOUT ARTIST: Donna Cozatchy
TECHNICAL DRAWINGS: Kevin Pierce

For over a quarter century, Kerry Pierce has specialized in post-and-rung chairmaking. He's the author of 10 woodworking books, including *The Art of Chair-Making*, *Making Elegant Gifts from Wood* and *The Custom Furniture Sourcebook*. Since 1995, he's served as contributing editor of *Woodwork* and is a frequent contributor to that magazine. His chairs have been exhibited at a number of Ohio venues, most recently at "Ohio Furniture by Contemporary Masters" at the Ohio Decorative Arts Center. He has also been a chairmaking instructor at the Marc Adams School of Woodworking.

ACKNOWLEDGEMENTS

One of the coolest things about writing books is this: The publisher actually gives you a page on which you can thank the people who have directed a little kindness your way. Here, in no particular order, is a list of some of the many people to whom I owe thanks.

John McDonald, past editor of *Woodwork* magazine, who got me into this business of writing about woodworking

John LaVine, the current editor of *Woodwork* magazine, whose continuing support has meant so much

Jim Stack, the acquisitions editor at Popular Woodworking Books, who has been both generous and encouraging ever since his arrival at F&W (I'm particularly grateful for the opportunity to do this book about Shaker furniture making)

The many good people at the Taunton Press, Sterling Publications, Lark Books and F&W, who have given me opportunities

The craftsmen I've interviewed over the last ten years, who have kindly shared their skills, in particular Charles Harvey, Joe Graham, David Wright, Judy Ditmer, Warren May, Craig Stevens, Rob Gartzka, Kathie Johnson, Brian Boggs, Mark Arnold, Mark Burhans and Joe Leonard (I wish I could say I remembered everything they demonstrated in their shops)

John Kassay and Ejner Handberg, whose books have provided me with information about most of the Shaker objects I build

Verne Ayers, a remarkably generous friend

My dad, Jim Pierce, who taught more than I managed to learn about craftsmanship and the importance of hard work

My mother, Sally Pierce, who taught me to read and to love books

My brother, Kevin, who has done the drawings for every single one of my project books (why do the drawings look so much better than the pieces I built?)

My wife, Elaine, whose patience and unqualified support have made my life possible

My daughter, Emily, and my son, Andy, who have given my life both purpose and direction

And, of course, the many Shaker craftsmen whose designs appear here on these pages.

TABLE OF CONTENTS

INTRODUCTION . . . 6

PROJECT ONE
14   sewing desk

PROJECT TWO
48   mount lebanon side chair

PROJECT THREE
70   union village rocker

PROJECT FOUR
80   transitional rocker

PROJECT FIVE
86   bentwood boxes and carriers

PROJECT SIX
98   tripod table

PROJECT SEVEN
108   hanging cupboard

PROJECT EIGHT
114   wall clock

PROJECT NINE
122   peg rail

PROJECT TEN
124   clothes hangers

SUPPLIERS . . . 126

INDEX . . . 127

Shaker Furniture for the 21st Century

T he number of American Shakers was never greater than 6,000 at any one time — a very small total for a sect looming so large in the public consciousness. And while many of the Shaker men and women accomplished rough work with wood, the number of Shakers producing fine furniture was likely only a small fraction of the total membership.

Yet today, more than a century after the zenith of Shaker furniture making has come and gone, when the number of practicing Shakers has been reduced to a mere handful, a search for "Shaker furniture" on the Google Internet search engine turns up over 65,000 hits, only a few of which refer to information about authentic Shaker furniture. Most, the overwhelming majority, refer to contemporary furniture that the makers (or sellers) describe as either Shaker reproduction or — more often — Shaker inspired. This is powerful evidence of the enduring appeal of Shaker woodworking.

Why should the work of this relatively obscure and historically distant religious sect exert such a profound influence on contemporary furniture mak-

ing? There are likely many answers.

Some of the attraction may be based on our admiration of a society that had institutionalized the rejection of materialism. Individual Shakers didn't own property. They didn't have private residences. They couldn't accumulate personal goods. Their beliefs forbid individual wealth. Instead, the focus in American Shaker communities was on service to God, to something larger and more important than themselves. In the avowedly materialistic 21st century America, in a country in which SUVs and annual vacations and air-conditioning are seen as minimum requirements for human happiness, in such a place, the Shakers' ascetic, other-directed lifestyle offers an appealing — if perhaps unrealistic — alternative, one in which meaning is more important than accumulation.

But Shaker furniture exists in the public consciousness in large part unrelated to the spiritual principles from which it initially flowed. For most of us, the word *Shaker*, when applied to furniture, carries a semantic weight similar to Queen Anne or Chippendale or Federal. It's a kind of furniture with characteristics different enough from other kinds of furniture so that those differences can be articulated by any knowledgeable student of furniture history. Maybe we don't know *why* it looks the way it looks, but we recognize it when we see it.

Another element in its appeal is the apparent technical simplicity Shaker furniture offers the contemporary maker. High-style, 18th-century furniture is intimidating to those who might want to replicate it. It demands that makers be well versed not only in cabinetmaking, but also in veneering and carving and turning. A craftsman unable to reproduce, for example, a veneered Federal table with turned and reeded legs might be able to reproduce a Shaker table of similar dimensions from the same approximate period, one demanding a less comprehensive set of skills because, at least on the surface, Shaker furniture appears to be but a small step forward from the simple country furniture in which it is rooted.

Bruce Cohen's chest of drawers is Shakeresque in its simplicity and directness, but the long curve in the plinth identifies the chest as a contemporary piece.

This towering chest of drawers made by Ian Ingersoll displays characteristics of the very best Shaker casework. First, notice the ten flights of drawers (a deliciously exaggerated number). Each flight is punctuated by a pair of walnut knobs and creates a strong rhythmic statement. Second, the piece is given a visual texture through the use of figured maple throughout.

But in actual fact, that step might be a large one. Consider Shaker chairmaking. That wasn't a discipline the Shakers created out of whole cloth. It was instead an evolution in the practice of chairmaking that had its origins in the country chairmaking of the period. The Shakers took the basic post-and-rung form, then in widespread use, and gave it a level of refined simplicity it hadn't previously known. They stripped away superfluous detail, attenuated posts and rungs, and lavished on every part a degree of intelligent care that the form rarely experienced outside the Shaker communities. Although the work of Shaker and country chairmakers did share a common ancestor, the end products were as different as orchids and dandelions.

Similarly, Shaker casework is related to, but different from, country casework. In both genres, forms are simple and direct, often severely geometrical. The case is a box with rectangular faces, and the drawers are let into openings cut into that box. The case usually stands on a simple plinth (or a simple set of legs) and is topped by a solid-wood panel whose only adornment is quite often a rounded edge. In the hands of a rough country workman, this form was often brutish and crude, but in the hands of a gifted Shaker craftsman, this form was given a presence rivaling that of high-style casework of the period.

Even the oval box, the quintessential expression of Shaker minimalism and elegance, isn't a Shaker invention. Similar bentwood boxes have a history reaching back for centuries. But here, too, the Shakers so forcefully put their stamp on a preexisting form that today, when we think of bentwood boxes, we automatically think of the Shakers.

When viewed from another perspective, the long shadow cast by a handful of Shaker craftsmen can be attributed to marketing. Contemporary craftsmen want to associate their work with the tradition of excellence ascribed to Shaker work. On the nuts-and-bolts level, however, this association can sometimes be difficult to see. If you look closely at some contemporary work described by its makers as Shaker-inspired, you may find it difficult to see any realistic Shaker connection. (My favorite Shaker malapropism, which appeared in a recent tool catalog, is a set of plans for a Shaker lingerie chest.) And in other cases, the word *Shaker* seems to be a kind of camouflage, a bit of verbal misdirection intended to encourage prospective buyers not to look too closely at rough and poorly conceived work, work in which the potential buyers are encouraged to see clumsiness as the equivalent of simplicity.

On the other hand, within the genre of Shaker-inspired contemporary furniture, you can also find breathtaking work in which the twin Shaker principles of minimalism and elegance are artfully conjoined, in which simplicity and meticulous construction are clearly evident. In some cases, this is work that more or less accurately reproduces a specific Shaker original. But in most cases, these gifted contemporary craftsmen are doing what their Shaker predecessors did themselves: They are reinventing contemporary forms in the enduring light of the Shaker sensibility.

Consider the Ian Ingersoll pine storage cabinet shown earlier in the introduction. This piece represents a very literal translation of Shaker cabinet-making principles. The use of pine as primary wood, the asymmetrical arrangement of drawers, the upper and lower compartments accessed only by a central frame and panel door — these are hallmarks of Shaker construction that Ingersoll has employed in the creation of a piece that is every bit as attractive and functional today as it would have been in the middle of the 19th century.

Compare that to the Bruce Cohen chest of drawers, also shown earlier in the introduction. Again, simplicity and directness of design are evident. The chest features two files of drawers with wood knobs set into a frame and panel cabinet, all characteristic of the best Shaker work, but Cohen has added a feature more typical of contemporary furniture than of classic Shaker work. Notice the long sweeping curve of the plinth. Details like this mark the piece as a 20th (or 21st) century piece.

Sometimes it's possible to breathe new life into an old form by making relatively minor changes. The Ian Ingersoll press cupboard (above) illustrates this point nicely. The Shaker original was made with solid-wood doors behind which the Shakers likely

This press cupboard built by Ian Ingersoll is — with the exception of the glass panel in each door — a faithful reproduction of a piece built in the late 19th century at the Pleasant Hill Shaker community.

Although this chair made by Ian Ingersoll exhibits characteristics of Shaker chairmaking — the tape seat and back, the turned posts and stretchers, the cushion rail — the net effect is clearly not Shaker.

This slat-back rocker originated in a New Lebanon chair drawn by John Kassay in *The Book of Shaker Furniture*.

stored linens. By substituting glass panels for wood, Ingersoll has transformed that original into something suited for the display of books or collectibles.

Plus, as the energetic tall chair (above, left) by Ian Ingersoll demonstrates, modern furniture makers sometimes create startlingly original work while employing recognizably Shaker motifs. Ingersoll's chair exhibits several Shaker characteristics — turned legs and stretchers, a cushion rail, and a seat and back woven of Shaker tape; however, the chair he created is clearly a modern construction. It is, in fact, a chair that might have forced Brother Robert

Wagan, the mastermind of the New Lebanon chairmaking operation, to do some serious head scratching. Yet it is a piece that today exists quite comfortably in Ingersoll's portfolio alongside other pieces that more accurately reproduce specific Shaker originals. It is both Shaker and not Shaker. It is a synthesis of the Shaker traditions in chairmaking and Ingersoll's modern sensibilities.

My own more modest experimentation with chair forms has produced several examples exhibiting details that are both Shaker and non-Shaker. The slat-back rocker (above, right) originated with a specific

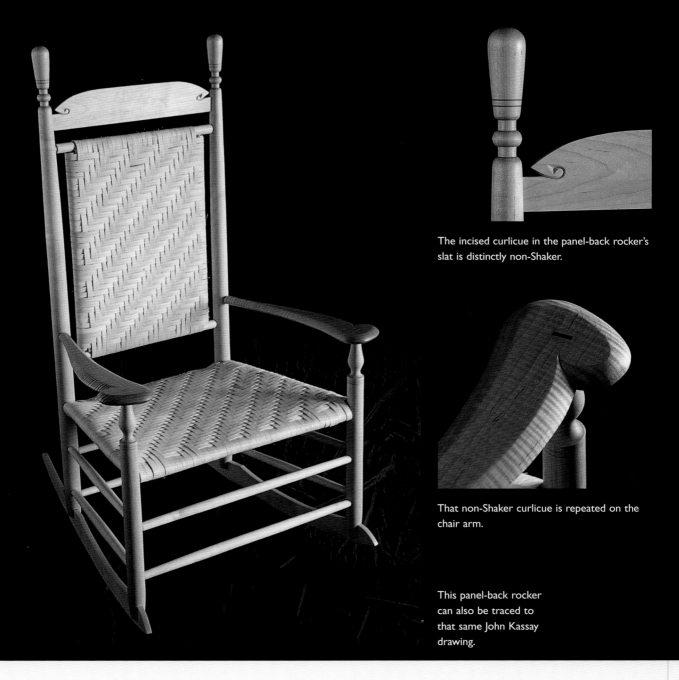

The incised curlicue in the panel-back rocker's slat is distinctly non-Shaker.

That non-Shaker curlicue is repeated on the chair arm.

This panel-back rocker can also be traced to that same John Kassay drawing.

Shaker chair, one drawn by John Kassay in *The Book of Shaker Furniture*. However, mine differs from the original in several key details. First, the back posts on the examples of this chair I've built over the last fifteen years have gradually moved closer together, giving the back a greater verticality. Second, the plain band-sawn arms of the original have been replaced by wider arms that have been sculpted to a distinctively non-Shaker form. And finally, the simple front-post tapers under each arm of the original have been replaced by vases, much like those appearing on other Shaker originals. Despite

these variations from the example drawn by John Kassay, this is a chair that many students of American furniture would likely identify as Shaker.

The panel-back rocker (above) is a different story, although it, too, is a variation of the same Shaker original. Like the original, it has rungs that taper from the center to shoulders at both ends. The back posts are simple rounds, tapering from the seat rung to a turned finial. Likewise, the front posts are simple rounds terminating in a vase just below each arm. And the rockers on my panel back are exactly the same as the rockers on the chair drawn by John

The simplicity and straightforward design of this bed made by Bruce Cohen reflect the principles of Shaker furniture making.

Kassay. This is a piece with many Shaker-inspired characteristics. What is not Shaker are the specific shapes of the finials, the wide sculpted arms, and the panel back woven around unbent false back posts. These differences result in a chair that is much less likely than my slat back to be identified as a Shaker piece.

The Shaker originals I've reproduced have influenced my work in at least two ways. First, the process of reproducing the originals has instructed me in construction techniques used in the creation of both chairs and casepieces. By recreating Shaker originals, I have learned how furniture can be assembled, and the importance of this technical instruction would be hard to overstate. But perhaps even more important is this: Reproducing dozens of Shaker originals has equipped me with a design vocabulary of forms, shapes and textures that has informed every Shaker and every non-Shaker piece I

now build.

Although the religious movement that gave birth to this genre of furniture making has contracted almost to the point of extinction, the influence of a handful of gifted 19th-century Shaker craftsmen continues to be felt in the Shaker originals still being reproduced and the many Shaker-inspired pieces being produced by contemporary craftsmen.

Will this influence continue to be felt throughout the 21st century?

The answer, I suspect, is yes. The key principles of Shaker furniture making — minimalism and elegance — will continue to feed the great river of American design, simply because these principles are too stylistically virtuous to disappear. Plus it's likely that a few stubborn retro makers, like myself, will continue to reproduce specific Shaker originals long into the new century if for no other reason than because we love them.

The Projects

None of the projects in the following chapters is absolutely faithful to the Shaker originals on which they are based. In many cases, I used different materials than the Shakers used. For example, for the sewing desk in project one I substituted cherry and poplar for the birch and pine in the original. In fact, I believe that the small cherry table in project six is the only piece made from the same material used by the Shakers in the construction of the original.

In other cases, changes were made to accommodate modern accessories. I built the clock in project eight, for instance, without a window in the side of the case. In the original clock, the viewing window provided access to the clock's intricate wooden movement. Such a window in my clock would reveal only the black plastic case of my electric movement.

In still other cases the changes were made for aesthetic reasons. For example, I have always thought that the Shaker-designed transition between post and tenon on the back posts of the rocker in project four — a taper leading into a sort of cove — was a bit awkward, so I used what I see as a more appealing transition. I don't mean to suggest that the designs of the Shaker originals were flawed; I mean only that, in some cases, they don't suit me.

And finally, in some cases changes were made for reasons I can't now identify. I've been making Shaker chairs for many years, and I know that some of the chairs I've built during those years have been adjusted over time to suit my tastes and my methods of construction. And I think that's the way things should be; that is, we should respect but not venerate the makers who came before us.

sewing desk

Although this is one of the simplest Shaker sewing desks I've ever seen, it is nevertheless a complex piece requiring many hours of shop time. I'm admittedly slow with large casepieces. Even so, I was surprised to learn that I had over 125 hours in the construction of this desk.

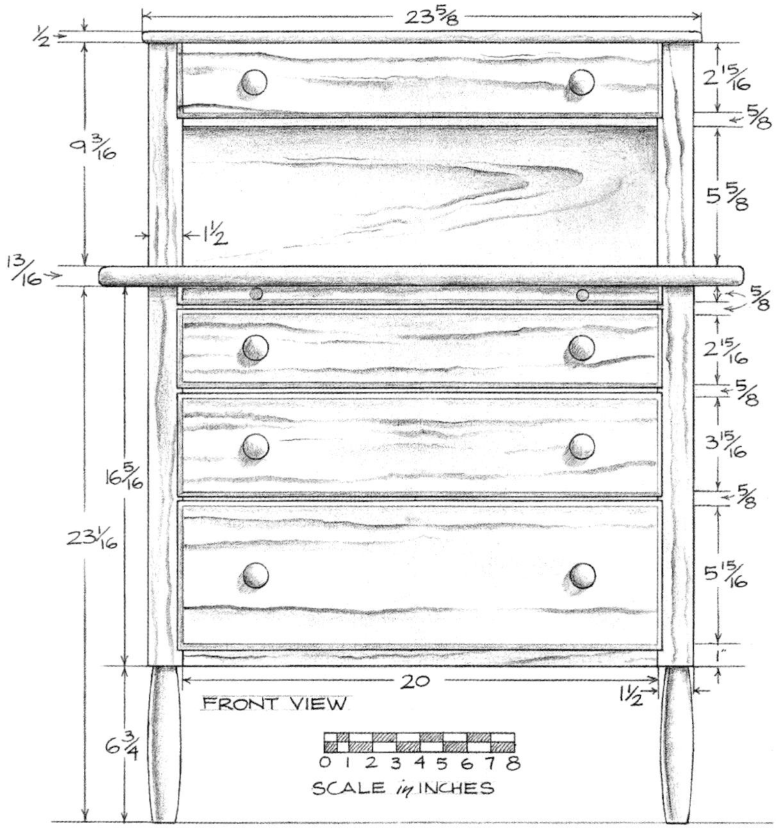
23 5/8
1/2
2 15/16
5/8
9 3/16
5 5/8
1 1/2
13/16
5/8
2 15/16
5/8
3 15/16
16 5/16
5/8
23 1/16
5 15/16
1"
20
1 1/2
FRONT VIEW
6 3/4
0 1 2 3 4 5 6 7 8
SCALE in INCHES

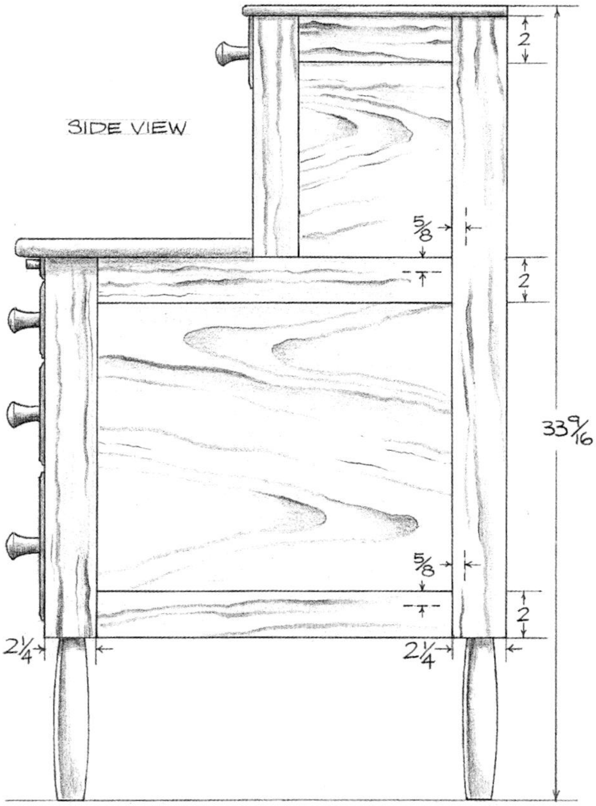
2
SIDE VIEW
5/8
2
33 9/16
5/8
2
2 1/4
2 1/4

UPPER TOP DRAWER

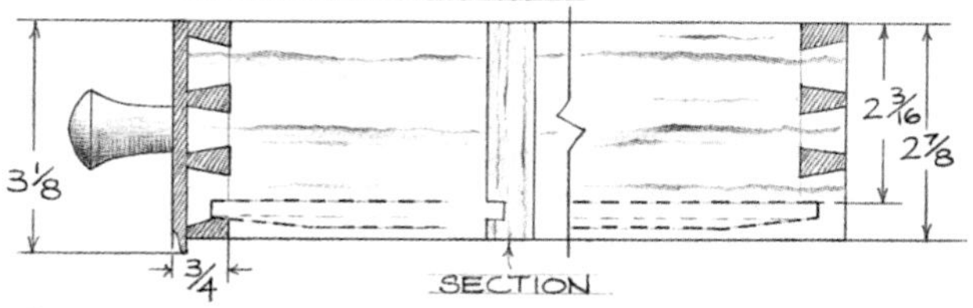
3 1/8
3/4
SECTION
2 3/16
2 7/8

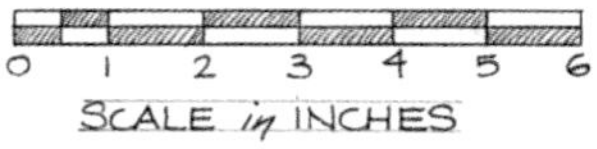
0 1 2 3 4 5 6
SCALE in INCHES

SLIDING SHELF

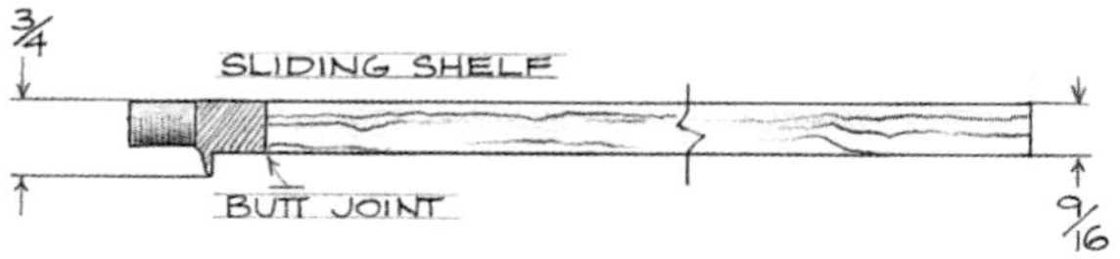
3/4
BUTT JOINT
9/16

SLIDING SHELF BACK VIEW

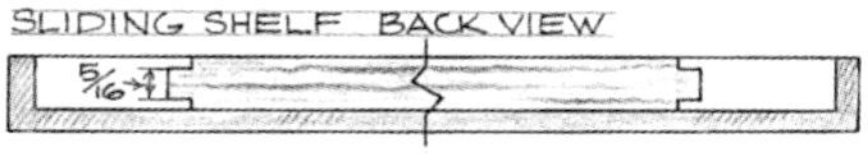
5/16

LOWER TOP DRAWER

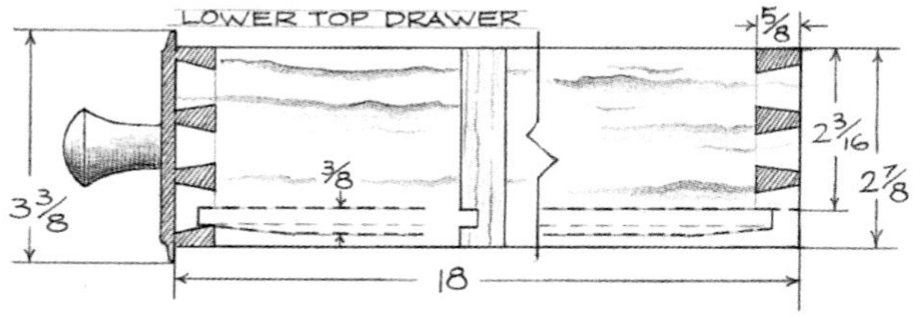
5/8
3 3/8
3/8
2 3/16
2 7/8
18

DRAWER FRONT VIEW

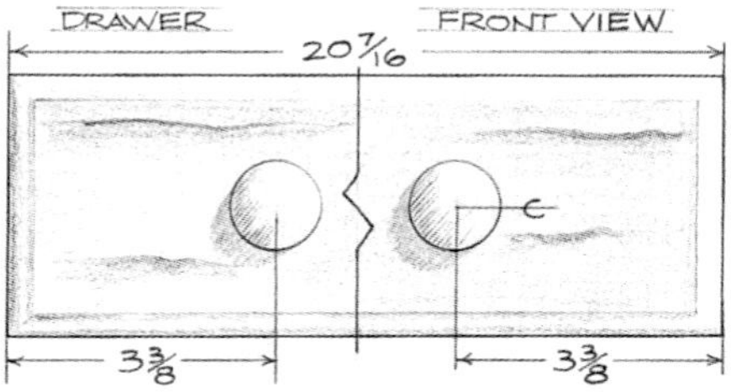
20 7/16
3 3/8
3 3/8

MIDDLE DRAWER

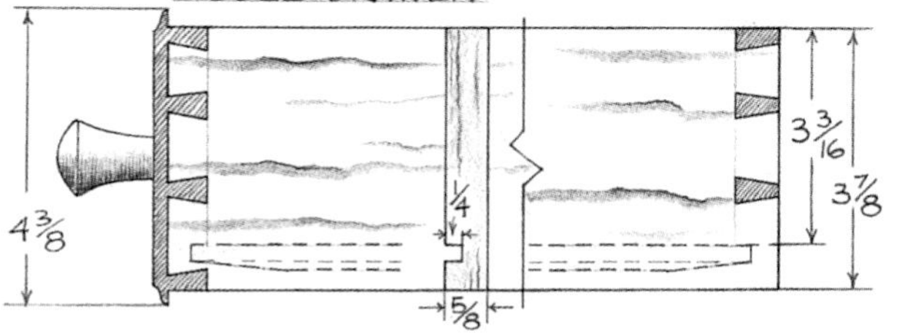
4 3/8
1/4
5/8
3 3/16
3 7/8

DRAWER BACK VIEW

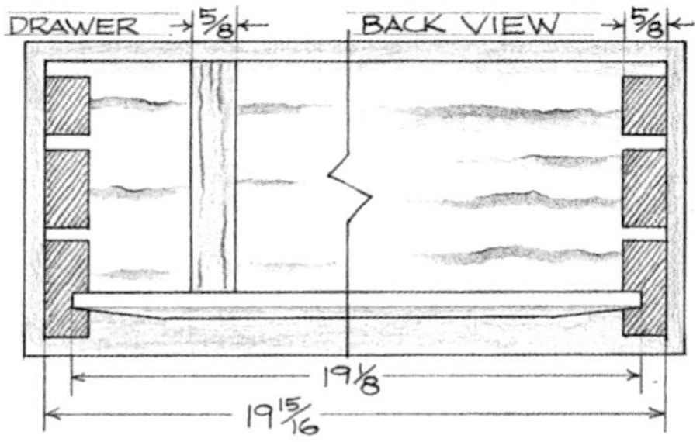
5/8
5/8
19 1/8
19 15/16

BOTTOM DRAWER

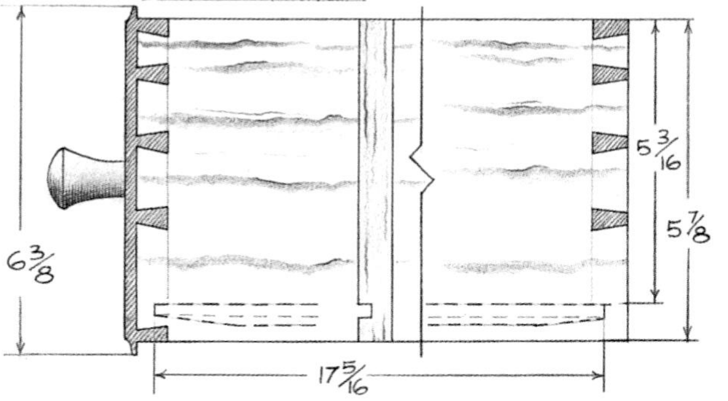
6 3/8
5 3/16
5 7/8
17 5/16

LOWER TOP DRAWER DETAIL

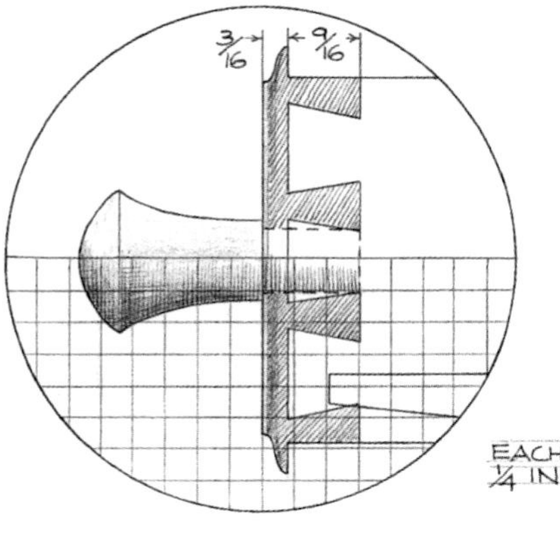
3/16
9/16

LEG DETAIL

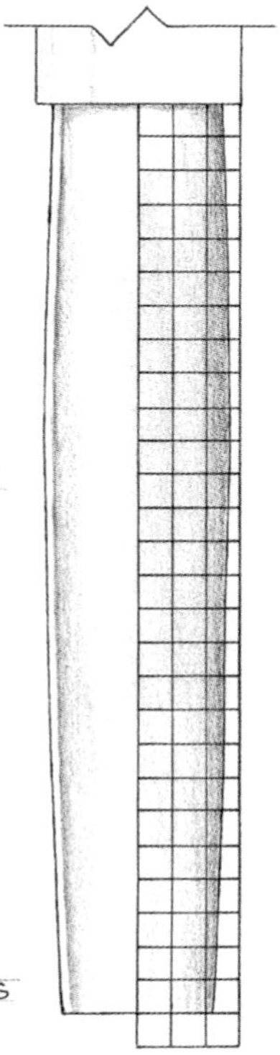

EACH GRID SQUARE REPRESENTS 1/4 INCH

inches (millimeters)

QUANTITY	PART	STOCK	THICKNESS	(mm)	WIDTH	(mm)	LENGTH	(mm)	COMMENTS
CASE									
2	back posts	cherry	$1^1/_2$	(38)	$2^1/_4$	(57)	$33^9/_{16}$	(852)	
2	front posts	cherry	$1^1/_2$	(38)	$2^1/_4$	(57)	$23^1/_{16}$	(586)	
2	short side stiles	cherry	$1^1/_4$	(32)	2	(51)	11	(279)	1" (25mm) tenon on bottom end
4	middle & bottom side rails	cherry	$1^1/_4$	(32)	2	(51)	17	(432)	1" (25mm) tenon on each end
2	top side rails	cherry	$1^1/_4$	(32)	2	(51)	$8^1/_2$	(216)	1" (25mm) tenon on each end
2	top side panels	cherry	$5/_{16}$	(8)	$9^1/_8$	(232)	$7^5/_8$	(194)	
2	bottom side panels	cherry	$5/_{16}$	(8)	$13^1/_2$	(343)	$16^1/_8$	(409)	
1	top back panel	cherry	$5/_{16}$	(8)	$9^1/_8$	(232)	$21^1/_8$	(536)	
1	bottom back panel	cherry	$5/_{16}$	(8)	$13^1/_2$	(343)	$21^1/_8$	(536)	
3	back rails	cherry	$1^5/_{16}$	(33)	2	(51)	22	(559)	1" (25mm) tenon on each end
1	bottom drawer rail	cherry	1	(25)	$1^1/_2$	(38)	22	(559)	1" (25mm) tenon on each end
3	lower middle rails	cherry	$5/_8$	(16)	$1^1/_2$	(38)	22	(559)	1" (25mm) tenon on each end
1	top drawer rail	cherry	$5/_8$	(16)	$1^1/_2$	(38)	$22^1/_2$	(572)	1" (25mm) tenon on each end
1	upper top	cherry	$1/_2$	(13)	$11^1/_4$	(285)	$23^5/_8$	(600)	
1	lower top	cherry	$3/_{16}$	(5)	$20^1/_2$	(520)	$27^1/_8$	(689)	
1	case bottom	poplar	$3/_8$	(10)	$16^1/_8$	(409)	$20^7/_{16}$	(519)	
8	lower drawer runners	poplar	$5/_8$	(16)	$1^5/_{16}$	(33)	$17^5/_{16}$	(440)	
8	lower drawer guides	poplar	$7/_{16}$	(11)	$1^1/_8$	(28)	$14^7/_8$	(378)	
2	bottom drawer guide filler strips	poplar	$1/_4$	(6)	$1/_2$	(13)	$14^7/_8$	(378)	
2	upper drawer runners	poplar	$5/_8$	(16)	$1^5/_{16}$	(33)	$8^5/_8$	(219)	
2	upper drawer guides	poplar	$7/_{16}$	(11)	$1^1/_8$	(28)	$6^1/_2$	(165)	
LOWER TOP DRAWER									
2	sides	poplar	$5/_8$	(16)	$2^7/_8$	(73)	18	(457)	
1	front	cherry	$3/_4$	(19)	$3^3/_8$	(86)	$20^7/_{16}$	(519)	
1	back	poplar	$5/_8$	(16)	$2^3/_{16}$	(56)	$19^{15}/_{16}$	(507)	
1	bottom	poplar	$3/_8$	(10)	$17^{15}/_{16}$	(456)	$19^7/_{16}$	(494)	
MIDDLE DRAWER									
2	sides	poplar	$5/_8$	(16)	$3^7/_8$	(98)	18	(457)	
1	back	poplar	$5/_8$	(16)	$3^3/_{16}$	(81)	$19^{15}/_{16}$	(507)	
1	front	cherry	$3/_4$	(19)	$4^3/_8$	(112)	$20^7/_{16}$	(519)	
1	bottom	poplar	$3/_8$	(10)	$17^{15}/_{16}$	(456)	$19^7/_{16}$	(494)	
BOTTOM DRAWER									
2	sides	poplar	$5/_8$	(16)	$5^7/_8$	(149)	18	(457)	
1	back	poplar	$5/_8$	(16)	$5^3/_{16}$	(132)	$19^{15}/_{16}$	(507)	
1	front	cherry	$3/_4$	(19)	$6^3/_8$	(162)	$20^7/_{16}$	(519)	
1	bottom	poplar	$3/_8$	(10)	$17^{15}/_{16}$	(456)	$19^7/_{16}$	(494)	
SLIDING SHELF									
1	front	cherry	$5/_8$	(16)	$2^7/_8$	(73)	$20^7/_{16}$	(519)	
1	center panel	poplar	$9/_{16}$	(14)	$16^1/_2$	(419)	$17^1/_4$	(438)	
2	breadboard ends	cherry	$9/_{16}$	(14)	2	(51)	$17^1/_8$	(435)	
2	knobs	cherry	$1/_2$ dia.	(13)	$1^3/_8$	(35)			
UPPER TOP DRAWER									
2	sides	poplar	$5/_8$	(16)	$2^7/_8$	(73)	$9^3/_8$	(239)	
1	back	poplar	$5/_8$	(16)	$2^3/_{16}$	(56)	$19^{15}/_{16}$	(507)	
1	front	cherry	$3/_4$	(19)	$3^1/_8$	(79)	$20^{15}/_{16}$	(532)	
1	bottom	poplar	$3/_8$	(10)	$9^1/_8$	(232)	$19^1/_4$	(489)	
8	knobs	cherry	$1^1/_8$ dia.	(28)			$2^3/_{16}$	(56)	

STEP 1 | Begin by selecting stock for the four posts. In this photo I've marked in pencil the approximate length of the posts I'll be ripping from this board.

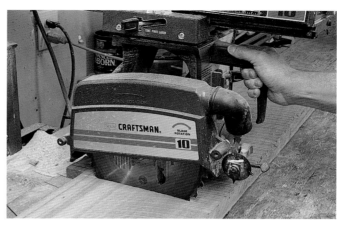

STEP 2 | Crosscut the material on your radial-arm saw. Remember that these lengths are only approximations, so the stock needs to be longer than your finished dimensions.

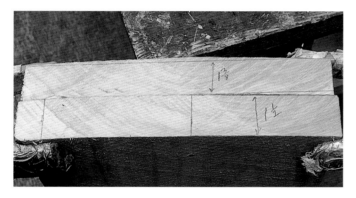

STEP 3 | Nearly all rough-sawn lumber is cupped. It's an inevitable part of the drying process. The method by which you choose to remove that cup will determine the thickness of the pieces you can take from your stock. The lines on the upper plank indicate the maximum thickness possible if the entire surface is flattened before it is ripped to width. The lines on the lower plank indicate the maximum possible thickness if the material is ripped in half before flattening.

hardware and supplies

2" (51mm) No. 12 wood screws
glue
1½" (38mm) No. 8 wood screws
brads
4d nails
wood screws

STEP 4 | Straighten one edge on your jointer. Notice that I'm not making any effort at this time to keep that straightened edge perpendicular to the face that butts the jointer fence. At this stage I want only to produce a straight edge I can hold against the fence on my table saw during the ripping process.

STEP 5 | Rip the material to approximate width. I've elected to rip the plank in two. From each of these halves I can later rip out two posts.

STEP 6 | Several passes over the jointer quickly flattens one face of each piece.

WARNING
• BE SURE THE CUTTER BLADE INS-
TALLATION BOLTS ARE SECURELY
TIGHTENED BEFORE OPERATING.
• KEEP HANDS AWAY FROM BLADES.

STEP 8 | Before jointing an edge on the properly thicknessed material, check to see that your jointer fence is 90° from the infeed and outfeed tables.

STEP 7 | Bring the material to its finished thickness using your planer. (I've set my planer so that it ejects shavings outside my shop's overhead door, onto the driveway where my son later scoops them up and hauls them away. In my view, this machine makes too much mess to use inside the shop.)

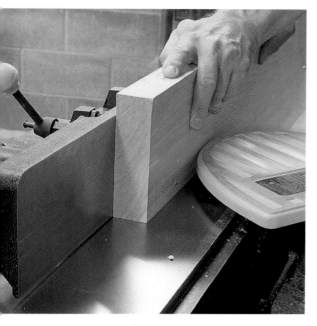

STEP 9 | Joint one edge. Notice that one face of the stock is kept pressed against the jointer fence to create two faces exactly 90° to each other.

STEP 10 | At this point, you're ready to rip the material to width. The edge jointed in step 9 is crowded against the table saw's rip fence. In order to end up with stock that finishes out to $2\frac{1}{4}$", rip it to $2\frac{5}{16}$". That will leave you with $\frac{1}{16}$" to remove when you clean up the saw marks on the newly sawn edge. (The blade guard has been removed for the purpose of this illustration. Never operate a table saw without a blade guard.)

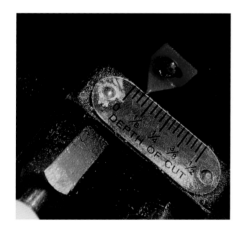

STEP 11 | Before jointing the sawn edge, check the gauge on your jointer to be sure that it's set to remove exactly $\frac{1}{16}$", then re-move that extra $\frac{1}{16}$".

STEP 12 | On your radial-arm saw, square up one end of the machined stock, then mark the length and cut to the final dimension. Note: These first 12 steps seem pretty boring, as they are simply materials preparation. However, speaking as a guy who in the past some-times glossed over these procedures, I can say — with the authority of too many failures — that accurate material preparation is the most critical part of any woodworking project. Remember, if you fudge here, you'll pay later.

STEP 13 | Carefully lay out the locations of the various mortises you'll be cutting in the posts. Then mark the centers for mounting in your lathe.

STEP 14 | Define the wider shoulders of the turned foot with your band saw. Notice the mortise laid out just above my right thumb. That mortise, I would later determine, is on the wrong edge. It should be down farther, under, rather than above my thumb. This is something I discovered during a later review of my layout.

STEP 15 | Define the narrower shoulders in the same way.

STEP 16 | Rip the surplus material from the wide sides of each foot, leaving a turning blank that is a square in cross section.

STEP 17 | With your roughing gouge, turn the feet into cylinders, taking care to stay away from the sawn shoulders.

STEP 18 | If you nick the sawn shoulders with a tool, the tool will be thrown, pretty violently, into the tool rest and maybe the work, as well. For that reason, I choose to nibble away at the material next to those shoulders with a parting tool. This isn't a very elegant turning method, but it does suit my cautious nature.

STEP 19 | Once you've removed the bulk of the material with your parting tool, you can peel away the little that remains with the point of your skew. Again, be wary of that sawn shoulder.

STEP 20 | Finish the turned foot with abrasives.

STEP 21 | Before I began cutting mortises I reviewed my layout work, discovering the goof I mentioned in step 14. This is what your layout work should look like.

STEP 22 | I have a ½" mortise chisel for my drill press, but it's such a cranky piece of equipment I chose to crumb out the waste with a series of holes made by a 7⁄16" Forstner bit and then go back and finish with a paring chisel. Notice the fence that aligns the center of each mortise.

STEP 23 | This close-up at one end of the fence shows that most of the material has been removed.

STEP 24 | You have to eliminate the fence when crumbing out the mortises for the drawer rails.

STEP 25 | With a knife, delineate the cross-grained ends of each mortise.

STEP 26 | A paring chisel will quickly transform those round $^7/_{16}$" holes into square $^1/_2$" mortises.

STEP 27 | Here are two completed mortises.

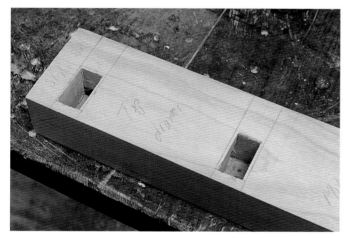

STEP 28 | After the mortises have been cut, it's time to plow the $^3/_8$" × $^1/_4$" grooves into which the case's six outside panels will be housed. Do this on your table saw using a dado cutter. (The blade guard has been removed for the purpose of this illustration. Never operate a table saw without a blade guard.)

STEP 29 | Some of the grooves have to be stopped in order to keep the dado cutter from digging into the turned foot. In this photo I've reached the end of my groove — indicated by a pencil line on the saw fence — and I'm lifting the post from the dado cutter after the saw has been shut off.

STEP 30 | In this photo you can just barely make out the pencil arrow sketched on the steel fence. When the square shoulder above the foot reaches this mark, it's time to shut off the saw and lift the post from the cutter.

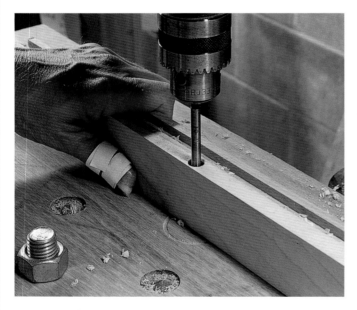

STEP 31 | The measured drawing in John Kassay's *The Book of Shaker Furniture*, on which this desk is loosely based, makes no mention of a method for fastening the tops. I considered several alternatives and settled on screw holes in the cross rails. First I drilled a ⅜" hole for the head. This hole should be set at a depth that will work with the screws you've chosen to fasten the top into place. (I selected 2" No. 12 wood screws.) You want the hole for the head to penetrate enough so that when the screw is placed into the through-hole you'll drill next, enough of the screw will protrude beyond that through-hole to firmly grip the top without allowing the screw to penetrate the surface of the top. It takes a little time to make it all work.

STEP 32 | Then, with a smaller bit — one big enough to allow the body of the screw to pass through — drill all the way through the rail stock.

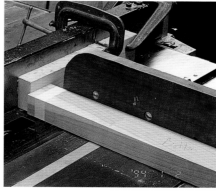

STEP 34 | The block clamped to the fence sets the length of the tenons.

STEP 33 | My dado cutter is an old-fashioned, stacked cutter that has a tendency to disturb wood fibers where the tenon shoulder meets the outside faces of the stock being tenoned. For that reason I wrap a layer of masking tape around the shoulder area. This reduces the amount of disturbance. If you have a dado head that cuts cleanly, you could skip this step.

STEP 35 | With the fence clamped in this location, place the end of the part against the block and then, holding that part tight against the miter gauge, slide it past the dado cutters. Although the depth of the tenon cheek is the same on the outside of each framing member, the depth of the tenon cheek on the inside is determined by the thickness of each individual element. In every case, enough material should be removed to leave behind a $\frac{1}{2}$"-thick tenon.

STEP 36 | The width of each tenon could also have been created using the stack of dado cutters. For this procedure, however, I opted to cut them with a backsaw. If you choose this method, mark the tenon width from the width of the mortise.

STEP 37 | Square down a line from each mark, then saw each tenon to width.

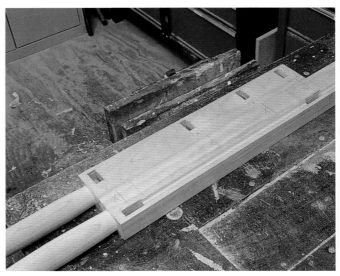

STEP 38 | Before assembling the case, lay out the locations of the drawer rails on the interior of the case.

STEP 39 | I always dry assemble the frame to check my layout. This procedure also gives me my first glimpse of the size of the finished piece.

STEP 40 | After resawing the panel stock to a $\frac{1}{2}$" thickness, flatten one side of each piece on your jointer.

STEP 41 | After thicknessing the stock in your planer, joint the edges you're about to glue.

STEP 42 | Lay out the jointed pieces to see that the edges come together nicely, without any gaps. I use the squiggly line to remind me how these are to be brought together during glue-up.

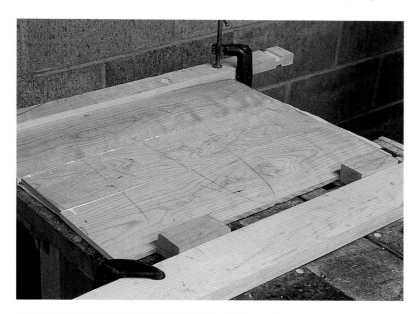

STEP 43 | Because it's difficult to hold thin stock in pipe or bar clamps, I recommend this method for gluing up these 3/8"-thick panels. Clamp a pair of cleats to the top of a bench, then position the glued-up pieces between those cleats.

STEP 44 | Apply pressure to the joints with two pairs of wedges, tapping each pair in until tight, as shown here.

STEP 45 | If the panels don't lie flat, apply some weight.

STEP 46 | Belt sanders are completely unsuitable for leveling glued-up panels, although they are often used for this purpose. A scraper, like the Stanley No. 80 I'm using here, removes material much more quickly, without creating the furrows for which belt sanders are notorious. And they have the added advantage of not creating any noise or dust.

STEP 47 | The scraper should be followed by a sanding block, working through a variety of grits: 80 (if you need it), 100, 150 and 220.

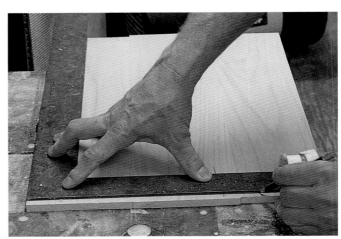

STEP 48 | The panel should then be marked for cutting.

STEP 50 | A small bevel along each edge will help the panel fit into the grooves you plowed in the posts and rails.

STEP 49 | The panel could also be ripped on the table saw, then cut to length on a radial-arm saw or on the table saw with a cutoff box.

STEP 51 | This close-up shows the completed bevels.

STEP 52 | Before gluing up a panel, make a dry run with all clamps, pads and a square. This allows you to resolve any problems before beginning the critical gluing process.

STEP 53 | After the panel has been glued up and after the glue has cured, remove the clamps and check to see how the joints came together. In this photo, one of the rails is coming into one of the posts with its surface slightly elevated.

STEP 54 | A little work with a block plane quickly levels these surfaces.

STEP 55 | A wash of paint thinner will show you how the joints will look after finish has been applied. If there are any gaps, fill them with a thick mixture of glue and sanding dust. Then, after the mixture has dried, sand it flat.

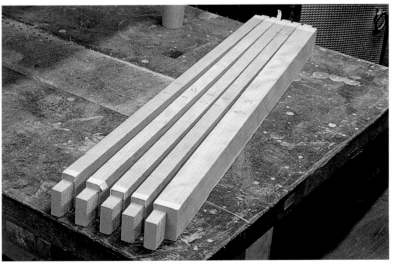

STEP 56 | The drawer rails should be ripped out, cut to length and tenoned.

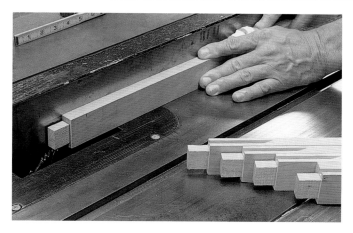

STEP 57 | Cut a short groove in the back edge of each end of each drawer rail. A tongue you will later cut on the drawer runners will fit into this groove.

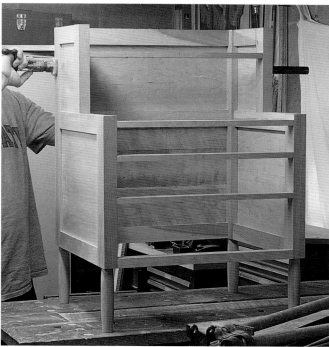

STEP 58 | Dry fit the case to ensure that everything comes together nicely.

STEP 59 | Check to see that the drawer rails and end panels come together at 90° angles. This is a check you should repeat regularly during the assembly process.

STEP 60 | Glue up the case. Use a number of pipe or bar clamps to hold all the joints tight while the glue cures. Allow it to sit overnight.

STEP 61 | Tack lengths of scrap across the corners to hold the case square during the curing process.

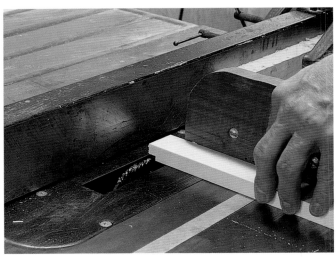

STEP 62 | Cut the tongues on one end of each drawer runner. These tongues will fit into the grooves you cut in step 57. This short runner will be used on the short drawer above the desk's lower top.

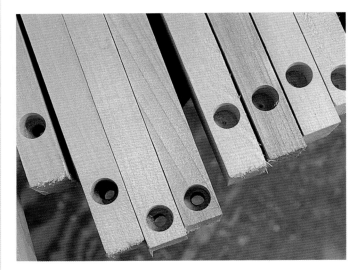

STEP 63 | Each runner will be held in place by a single screw passing through the end of the runner opposite the tongue. The runners on the right have been drilled to receive the head of the 1½" No. 8 wood screw. The runners on the left have also been drilled to receive the shank of that screw.

STEP 64 | Attach the drawer guides to each runner.

STEP 65 | This photo shows two runners with drawer guides attached and fastened into place.

STEP 66 | The screw fastening each runner is turned into the rear post.

STEP 67 | Because the short stiles alongside the uppermost drawer are thinner than the back post, the drawer runners require a small spacing block before they're pinned into place.

STEP 68 | Once the runners have been positioned, fasten them with a brad tapped through a predrilled hole into the tongue at the front end of each runner. This keeps the tenon at the end of the runner from sliding in its mortise.

STEP 69 | Glue up the desk's lower top. First, joint the edges of the boards, then dry clamp them to check alignment and clamp placement (as shown here). Glue them together and allow them to sit in clamps overnight.

STEP 70 | A little work with a scraper quickly levels these surfaces. Finish with sanding blocks as you did when leveling the panels for the outside of the case.

STEP 71 | Rip the panel to width.

STEP 72 | Remove saw marks by passing the sawn edges over your jointer.

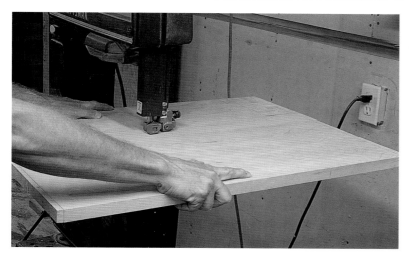

STEP 73 | Cut the panel into two sections, then joint these edges.

STEP 74 | This photo shows how the two parts of the lower top will come together.

STEP 75 | This photo shows the same corner as is shown in the previous step, after the desk has been completed.

STEP 76 | Joint the mating edges of the two parts of the lower top. Then dry clamp to check their alignment.

STEP 77 | With a scratch awl, mark the locations of the screw holes you made in steps 31 and 32.

STEP 78 | Remove the front part of the lower top and round its front and side edges with your router.

STEP 79 | Glue the edges of both parts of the lower top and clamp them together as you did in step 76. Then, after the glue has cured, fasten the lower top into place with the 2" No. 12 wood screws.

STEP 80 | Install ½" × ½" cleats on the inside of the desk's back and front. These cleats will receive the screws that will hold the case bottom in place.

STEP 81 | Fit the case bottom around each of the posts.

STEP 82 | Fit but don't fasten the case bottom. (I find it's easier to complete all the interior work before fastening the bottom in place.)

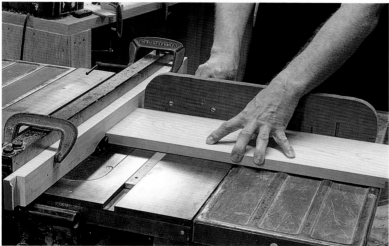

STEP 83 | After ripping the drawer fronts to width and cutting them to length, create a cabinet lip all around with a stack of dado cutters buried in a piece of scrap so that only the desired amount of cutter is exposed. First, cut the lips on the ends of the drawer front, using a miter gauge to help control the stock as it's passed over the cutters.

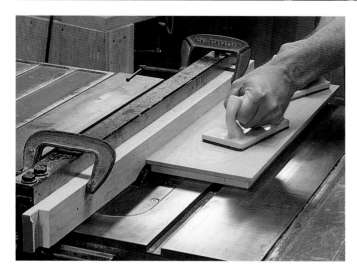

STEP 84 | Then cut the lips on the sides of the drawer front.

STEP 85 | On your router table, create the moulded edge around the face of each drawer front. Begin by cutting the edge on the ends of the fronts (note the use of the miter gauge). Then cut the edges on the sides of the fronts.

STEP 86 | I try to cut the cabinet lips on the back sides of each drawer front so that the front will fit snugly into its opening. When the end grain is pared down after drawer assembly, a bit of clearance is created at each side of the drawer. The tape shown here isn't really necessary because each front is fit pretty tightly.

STEP 87 | After the drawer sides have been thicknessed, ripped to width and cut to length, plow a ¼" × ¼" groove in each part to accept the edges of the drawer bottoms.

STEP 88 | The four parts for one drawer can be seen here. Notice that the drawer back (lying on the back side of the drawer front) and the space between the lips on the drawer front are the same length. Notice also that the drawer back has no groove. That's because it won't extend below the top surface of the drawer bottom.

STEP 89 | Before you begin dovetailing a drawer, be sure you number both parts of each corner. That way you won't get caught trying to fit together the wrong parts.

STEP 90 | Carefully mark with a knife, as I'm doing, or a marking gauge, the depths of the various parts of the dovetails. Most parts are marked $\frac{5}{8}$" from the end of the part because the sides and back have been planed $\frac{1}{32}$" less than $\frac{5}{8}$". The front corner of each side piece is marked $\frac{1}{2}$" from the end because the cabinet lip on the drawer front is only $\frac{1}{2}$" deep.

STEP 91 | After squaring lines across the end grain of the drawer sides, cut the sides of each tail. I do this freehand, without previously marking the angles. The marks shown here are sketched for the purposes of illustration. As you can see, I'm not making any particular effort to keep to those lines.

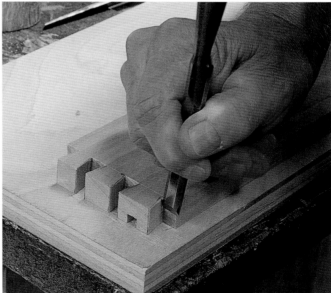

STEP 92 | With a coping saw, remove the waste between the tails. Be careful not to approach the scored line too closely.

STEP 93 | Clamp the drawer side to a piece of scrap on your bench, then pare down to the scored line, working from both sides toward the middle.

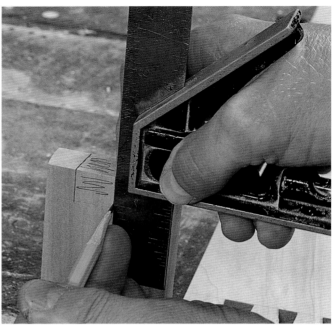

STEP 94 | Clamp the drawer back in your vise. Position the drawer side on the end grain of the drawer back and very carefully mark the limits of each tail on the end grain of the drawer side.

STEP 95 | Connect the pencil lines on the end grain with the scored line using your try square.

STEP 96 | Use a backsaw to define the sides of each pin. Be sure you're cutting on the waste side of the line.

STEP 97 | Use a paring chisel to clean up the spaces between pins just as you did when cleaning up the spaces between tails, then fit the joint.

STEP 98 | Clamp the drawer front in your vise, then place the drawer side on top of the rabbet, behind the lip, and mark the limits of each tail on the end grain of the drawer side.

STEP 99 | Once again, use the try square to connect the pencil lines on the end grain with the scored line.

STEP 100 | Use chisels to chop out the waste between pins. The masking tape is there to protect the back side of the lip in case the chisel slips.

STEP 101 | Use a paring chisel to clean up the openings that will house the tails. Notice that the protective masking tape has been removed.

STEP 102 | Carefully fit the joint. (Before gluing up the drawers, be sure to drill the mortises for the knob tenons. This is most accurately done on the drill press.) Once the mortises have been drilled and all four sets of dovetails are cut, glue up the drawers, checking each one with a framing square before setting it aside to dry.

STEP 103 | The protruding pins can be leveled with a plane or a rasp.

STEP 104 | After the drawer bottom material has been thicknessed and joined, rip it to width and cut it to length. Then mark the thickness of the ends of the bevel on the front and sides of the drawer bottom.

STEP 105 | With a jack plane, create the bevels that will allow the drawer bottom to slide into its grooves in the drawer front and drawer sides.

STEP 106 | The bottom can be held in place with a couple of 4d nails.

STEP 107 | A neatly fit set of dovetails makes a strong visual accent.

STEP 108 | The slide-out shelf is assembled around a tongue set into a groove in a pair of breadboard ends. Create the tongue with a couple of passes over a set of dado blades.

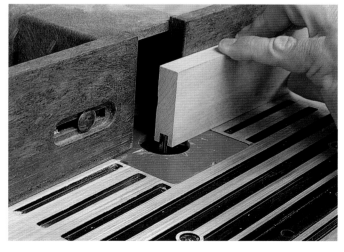

STEP 109 | Use a router bit to cut the grooves in the breadboard ends.

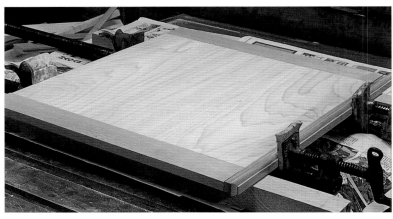

STEP 110 | The breadboard ends are held in place by the snugness of the groove. I also added a single drop of glue in the center of the main panel's width. This bit of glue will hold the ends in place while allowing the main panel to expand and contract across its width.

STEP 111 | After the breadboard ends have been glued in place, glue the shelf front to the main panel. Notice that the breadboard ends are recessed slightly from the front edge of the main panel. This allows the main panel to shrink without popping off the drawer front.

STEP 112 | Prepare the turning blanks for the knobs.

STEP 113 | Turn the blank into a cylinder with your roughing gouge.

STEP 114 | Create the top of each knob by placing the tip of your skew on the stock and rolling the skew so that it slices down. Several passes will be necessary.

STEP 115 | Create the lower surface of each knob with your fingernail gouge.

STEP 116 | Form the tenon at the base of each knob with a butt chisel laid bevel-side down on your tool rest.

STEP 117 | Glue the tenons into their mortises.

STEP 118 | Now that the interior work has been completed, the case bottom can be screwed into place. The case is then ready for finishing.

2

mount lebanon side chair

This chair, based on the No. 6 side chair made in the Shaker chairworks at Mount Lebanon, was among the largest side chairs built by the Shakers, which makes it a pretty good fit for the average 21st-century American.

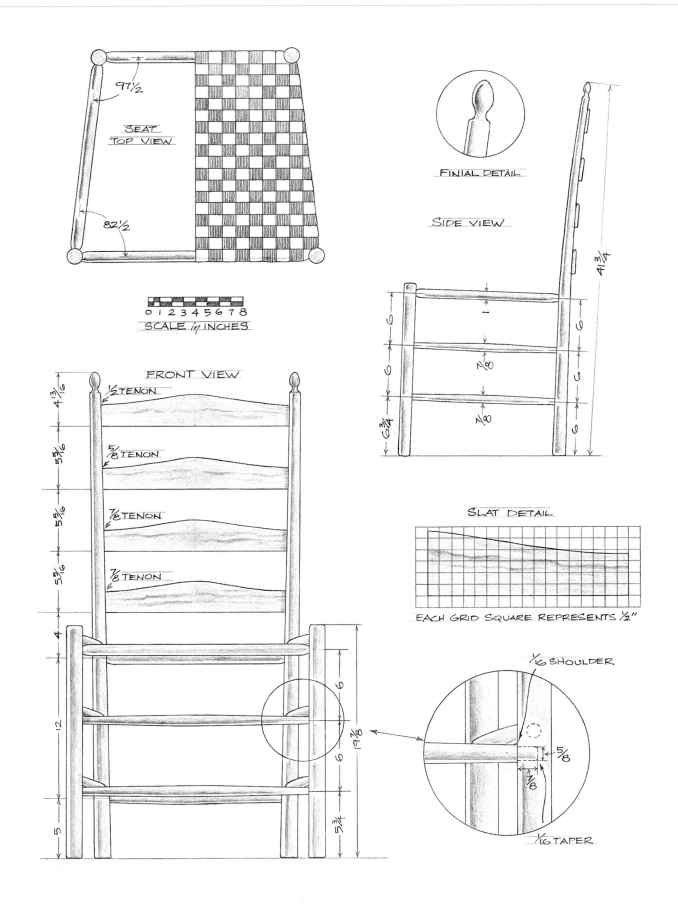

SEAT
TOP VIEW

$97\frac{1}{2}$

$82\frac{1}{2}$

0 1 2 3 4 5 6 7 8
SCALE in INCHES

FINIAL DETAIL

SIDE VIEW

$41\frac{3}{4}$

6

6

1

6

6

$1\frac{1}{8}$

6

$6\frac{3}{4}$

$1\frac{1}{8}$

6

FRONT VIEW

$4\frac{13}{16}$

$\frac{1}{2}$ TENON

$5\frac{5}{16}$

$\frac{5}{8}$ TENON

$5\frac{5}{16}$

$\frac{7}{8}$ TENON

$5\frac{5}{16}$

$\frac{7}{8}$ TENON

4

12

5

6

6

$19\frac{7}{8}$

$5\frac{3}{4}$

SLAT DETAIL

EACH GRID SQUARE REPRESENTS $\frac{1}{2}$"

$\frac{1}{16}$ SHOULDER

$\frac{5}{8}$

$\frac{7}{8}$

$\frac{1}{16}$ TAPER

50

Side Rung Mortise Jig

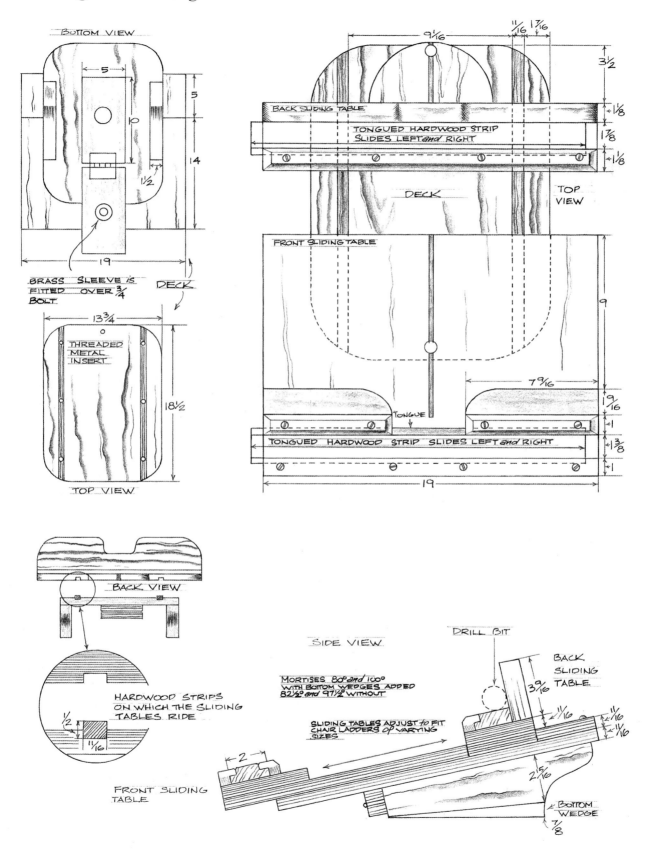

BOTTOM VIEW

5

5

10

14

1/2

19

BRASS SLEEVE is FITTED OVER 3/4 BOLT

DECK

13 3/4

THREADED METAL INSERT

18 1/2

TOP VIEW

9 1/16

11/16   1 7/16

3 1/2

BACK SLIDING TABLE

TONGUED HARDWOOD STRIP SLIDES LEFT and RIGHT

1/8

1 7/8

1/8

DECK

TOP VIEW

FRONT SLIDING TABLE

9

7 9/16

1 9/16

TONGUE

1

TONGUED HARDWOOD STRIP SLIDES LEFT and RIGHT

1 3/8

1

19

BACK VIEW

HARDWOOD STRIPS ON WHICH THE SLIDING TABLES RIDE

1/2

11/16

FRONT SLIDING TABLE

SIDE VIEW

DRILL BIT

BACK SLIDING TABLE

MORTISES 80° and 100° WITH BOTTOM WEDGES ADDED 82 1/2° and 97 1/2° WITHOUT

SLIDING TABLES ADJUST to FIT CHAIR LADDERS of VARYING SIZES

3 9/16

11/16

11/16

11/16

2

2 5/16

BOTTOM WEDGE

7/8

EACH GRID SQUARE REPRESENTS 1 INCH

PROFILE

EDGE VIEW

33

1½

EACH GRID SQUARE REPRESENTS 1 INCH

19⅝

4½

Front-Rung Mortise Jig

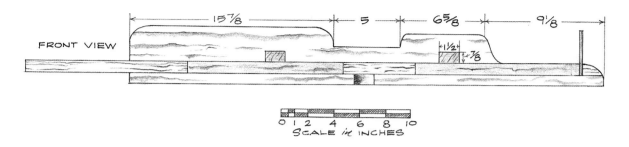

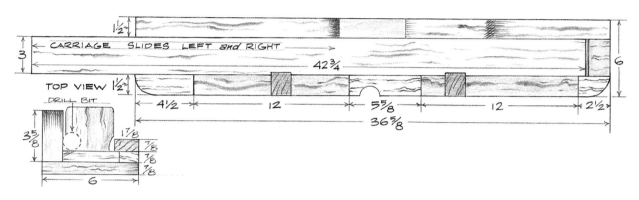

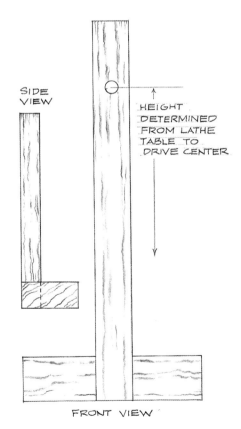

FRONT-RUNG MORTISE JIG • inches (millimeters)

QUANTITY	PART	STOCK	THICKNESS	(mm)	WIDTH	(mm)	LENGTH	(mm)
1	base	pine	7/8	(22)	6	(152)	36 5/8	(930)
1	sliding table	pine	13/16	(21)	3	(76)	42 3/4	(1086)
1	fence	pine	1 1/2	(38)	3 5/8	(92)	36 5/8	(930)
2	cleats	pine	7/8	(22)	1 1/2	(38)	12	(305)
2	guide blocks	pine	7/8	(22)	1 1/2	(38)	1 7/8	(47)
1	tail piece	pine	1/4	(6)	2 3/8	(61)	4	(102)

NOTE: The measurements given aren't critcal. Thicknesses, for example, are the thicknesses of material I had at hand on the day I made the jig.

SIDE CHAIR • inches (millimeters)

QUANTITY	PART	STOCK	THICKNESS	(mm)	WIDTH	(mm)	LENGTH	(mm)	COMMENTS
2	front posts	curly maple	1^7/$_{16}$ dia.	(36)			19^7/$_8$	(505)	
2	back posts	curly maple	1^7/$_{16}$ dia.	(36)			41^3/$_4$	(1060)	
3	front rungs	curly maple	^{15}/$_{16}$ dia.	(24)			20^3/$_4$	(527)	
6	side rungs	curly maple	^{7}/$_8$ dia.	(22)			17^3/$_4$	(451)	
2	back rungs	curly maple	^{7}/$_8$ dia.	(22)			16^1/$_4$	(412)	
1	top slat	curly maple	^{1}/$_4$	(6)	2^3/$_4$	(70)	16^7/$_8$	(428)	^{1}/$_4$" (6mm) tenon each end
1	upper middle slat	curly maple	^{1}/$_4$	(6)	2^3/$_4$	(70)	16^7/$_8$	(428)	^{5}/$_8$" (11mm) tenon each end
1	lower middle slat	curly maple	^{1}/$_4$	(6)	2^3/$_4$	(70)	16^7/$_8$	(428)	^{7}/$_8$" (22mm) tenon each end
1	bottom slat	curly maple	^{1}/$_4$	(6)	2^3/$_4$	(70)	16^1/$_2$	(419)	^{7}/$_8$" (22mm) tenon each end

NOTE: Seat rungs don't require the center-to-shoulder taper you cut in the show rungs. I leave these thicker, even if that means leaving a flat spot on one side (turned to the inside at assembly). The extra rung material gives the seat more strength. Plus, since the seat rungs are covered with splint or Shaker tape, there are no cosmetic reasons not to retain the extra material. Shaker tape can be purchased in a variety of colors from the Caning Shop (see Suppliers at the end of the book). In addition, the Caning Shop's Web site gives you a quick and easy way to figure the amount of tape required to seat this or any other chair. (This chair requires 140' of 1"-wide Shaker tape.)

SIDE RUNG MORTISE JIG • inches (millimeters)

QUANTITY	PART	STOCK	THICKNESS	(mm)	WIDTH	(mm)	LENGTH	(mm)	COMMENTS
DECK									
1	plywood deck	pine	^{3}/$_4$	(19)	13^3/$_4$	(349)	18^1/$_2$	(470)	
2	hardwood strips	pine	^{1}/$_2$	(13)	^{11}/$_{16}$	(18)	18^1/$_2$	(470)	
2	deck supports	pine	1^1/$_2$	(38)	3	(76)	12^3/$_4$	(324)	
2	leaves of plywood hinge	pine	^{3}/$_4$	(19)	5	(127)	10	(254)	
1	brass sleeve	pine	sized to fit snugly over bolt in table						
BACK TABLE									
1	plywood base	pine	^{3}/$_4$	(19)	7^7/$_{16}$	(189)	19	(483)	
1	plywood riser	pine	^{3}/$_4$	(19)	7^7/$_{16}$	(189)	19	(483)	
1	fence	pine	1^1/$_8$	(28)	3^9/$_{16}$	(90)	19	(483)	
1	tongued hardwood strip	pine	^{7}/$_8$	(22)	1^7/$_8$	(47)	19	(483)	
2	rabbeted hardwood strips	pine	^{7}/$_8$	(22)	1	(25)	7^1/$_8$	(181)	
FRONT TABLE									
1	plywood base	pine	^{3}/$_4$	(19)	14	(356)	9	(229)	
1	plywood riser	pine	^{3}/$_4$	(19)	5	(127)	19	(483)	
1	tongued hardwood strip	pine	^{7}/$_8$	(22)	1	(25)	19	(483)	
2	rabbeted hardwood strips	pine	^{7}/$_8$	(22)	1	(25)	7^1/$_2$	(191)	
1	rabbeted hardwood strip	pine	^{7}/$_8$	(22)	1	(25)	19	(483)	

NOTE: The measurements of this jig may have to be adapted to suit the size of your drill press table.

STEP 1 | If your pockets are deep enough, you can buy a lathe ready-made with enough distance between centers to turn a back post. But if, like me, your pockets are shallow, you may want to consider an alternative. This particular alternative involves a Craftsman lathe for which I paid $220 new. I removed the tubular lathe bed from the head stock, purchased a second mounting foot (just like the one on the tail-stock end of the lathe bed) and moved the whole bed far enough down my table to allow the necessary space between centers.

STEP 2 | My lathe table consists of 2×6s lag-screwed to the tops of two wood columns, each of which is filled with a couple of hundred pounds of gravel. This gives me a pretty stable turning platform.

STEP 3 | Begin by ripping out clear, straight-grained 1⅝" × 1⅝" turning blanks. Once you've ripped these blanks from larger stock, you may notice the stock bowing or twisting. These defects must be corrected on the jointer before marking the centers on each end.

STEP 4 | Center the turning stock on your band saw. I lay one corner in the notch in front of the blade and push the stock against the blade. I then rotate the stock 90° and repeat.

STEP 5 | This jig will allow you to turn square turning blanks into octagons, making the roughing process much less stressful.

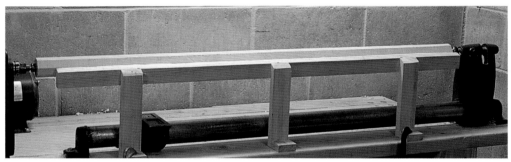

STEP 6 | The next step in my (idiosyncratic) method involves the use of wood length-of-part tool rests. These are not essential, because you can always slide a short rest along your lathe bed, but I don't think anyone who turns with these long rests will want to return to shorter ones.

STEP 7 | The back posts are very long and thin. When you press a gouge or a skew against this long, thin spindle it flexes away from the tool and bounces against the cutting edge, resulting in chatter. Sometimes this chatter is expressed in a pock-marked surface. Sometimes it is expressed in deep cuts that spiral around the spindle. In order to avoid this, you need to overcome the spindle's tenden-

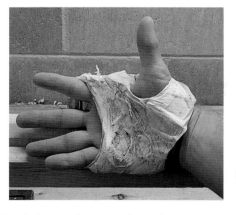

cy to flex away from the tool. Good technique and sharp tools are important. Lathe speed also matters. I've found a very slow speed exacerbates the flexing. But the most important part of the process involves the use of a steady rest. You can buy or make steady rests that can be moved along the lathe bed, but I've found the best steady rest is the one hanging from the end of my right arm. To protect my hand from friction burns, I wrap it in several layers of masking tape. Then, with my fingers pointed down so that they aren't drawn up into the gap between the spindle and the bottom edge of the tool rest, I lay the palm of my hand on the back side of the spindle. I then exert against the back side of the spindle a force equal to the force my tool is exerting on the front side of the spindle. This must be done carefully because if you press against the work with an unprotected area of flesh, it will heat up very quickly.

STEP 8 | With your roughing gouge, convert the eight-sided turning blank into a cylinder.

STEP 9 | Continue working with the roughing gouge until the post has been reduced to its finished diameters. Then, if you're comfortable with skew planing, plane the surface. A safer alternative is to use the skew as a scraper to clean up the ripples left by the gouge.

STEP 10 | Create the cove at the base of the acorn finial with a ¼" fingernail gouge.

STEP 11 | Sand the post through a variety of grits. I begin with 80, followed by 100, 150 and 220.

STEP 12 | The indexing head on my lathe is locked in place through the use of this spring-loaded pin, which can be released into 36 evenly distributed holes around the circumference of the head. That means that the distance between any two of those holes is 10°. After choosing which face of the post you want to show, lock the indexing head in place with the pin as shown here.

STEP 13 | This simple jig will allow you to mark a straight line, parallel to the center line of the spindle. (The pencil point is set to a height equal to the distance from the top of the lathe table to the center point of the lathe's drive center.) After marking the first line, rotate the post past 10 clicks on the lathe's indexing head and draw a second line. These two lines will then be 100° apart on the post's circumference. (In actual fact, the center lines of the back rungs and the side rungs on this particular chair are 97½° apart. However, placing them 100° apart at this stage in the process is close enough. The side-rung mortise jig will produce the final angles.) Use this same process to mark the front-rung mortises on the front posts, with one small difference. These lines should be separated by 8 clicks on the lathe's indexing head. (In actual fact, the center lines of the front rungs and the center lines of the side rungs are 82½° apart. Once again, the front-rung mortise jig will produce the final angles.)

STEP 14 | Lay your story stick on the spindle and mark the locations of all the back rung and back slat mortises along one of the lines you just made.

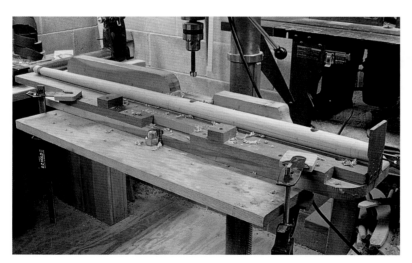

STEP 15 | Place the post on the front-rung mortising jig. Notice the jig's sliding table, which allows you to pass the post to the left and right under the drill bit. The fence of the jig should be placed a distance from the lead point on the drill bit that is half the greatest diameter of the post.

STEP 16 | To prevent the post from rotating as it is passed under the drill bit, turn a couple of screws through the sliding table's tail piece and into the end grain of the post. It isn't necessary to go very deep into the end grain; a couple of turns will do. After boring the back-rung mortises in the back posts, use this same jig and setup to bore the front-rung mortises on the front posts.

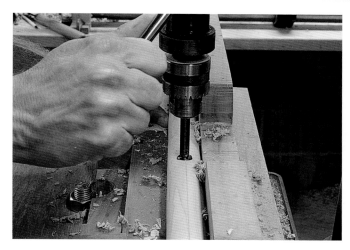

STEP 17 | After setting the stop on your drill press so that you will bore a hole ¹⁵⁄₁₆" deep, bring the Forstner bit into the post. (Forstner bits are notorious for poor chip ejection. To avoid burning the bit, bore the hole in several passes, raising the bit from the work after each pass to give chips a chance to clear.)

STEP 18 | After thicknessing the slat stock, cut the shape on your band saw. Then clamp each slat in your vise and remove the band saw marks. This can be done with a spokeshave, as I'm doing here, or it can be done with a rasp.

STEP 19 | A rasp is a slower but safer option.

STEP 20 | To clean up planer tear-out, use a sharp, wide butt chisel as a scraper to remove thin shavings from the torn-out surfaces of each slat.

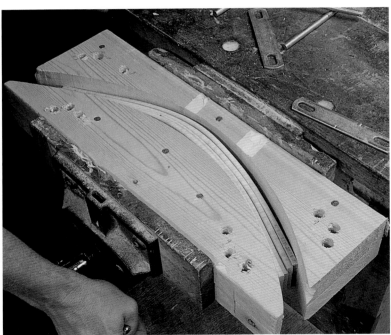

STEP 21 | The back posts and the slats need to be steamed before they're placed in the bending forms. The slats should be steamed for 30 minutes, while the posts require 90 minutes. My homemade steamer is built around a deep fryer that I bought at a garage sale, which, when filled with water, produces a generous amount of steam. The steam chamber is a length of 4" polyvinyl chloride (PVC) fit into a hole cut in the lid of the deep fryer. This length of PVC is clamped to a stepladder to keep it upright.

STEP 22 | After the slats have been steamed, use a vise to clamp the stack between the two halves of your bending form.

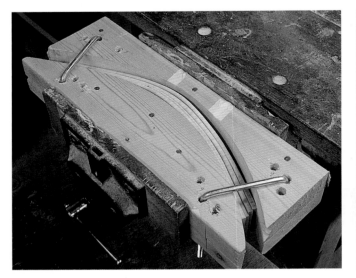

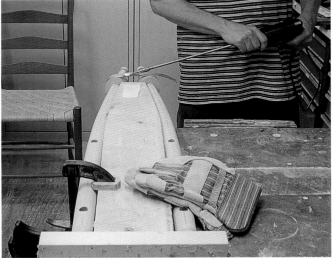

STEP 23 | To hold the two halves of the bending form together, drop a pair of U-bolts into the predrilled holes. Then slide the flat washers shown in the previous photo onto the legs of each U-bolt from underneath. The form can then be taken from the vise. The other holes are positioned to allow me to clamp either five or six slats in one bending form.

STEP 24 | The posts are then placed in a bending form with the back-rung holes facing up and the markings for the side-rung mortises facing out, to the left and right. The posts are given a bend through the use of a large hose clamp I tighten with an electric drill, fitted with a bit extender. You can do this without the bit extender, but if you do, the hose clamp will scuff up your drill chuck.

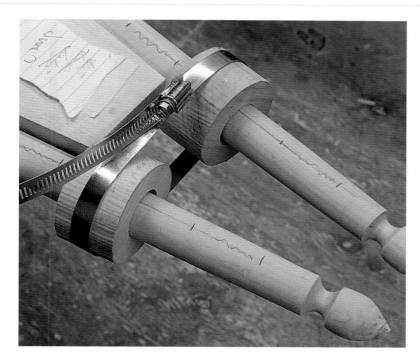

STEP 25 | This close-up shows the hose clamp and the protective wood collars on which the hose clamp rides. Notice the incompletely formed finials. They will be cleaned up with a rasp and sandpaper after the posts are removed from the bending form.

STEP 26 | I use wood length-of-part tool rests for the rungs, also.

STEP 27 | Mark the locations of the rung tenons directly on the tool rest.

STEP 28 | With a roughing gouge, convert the turning blank to a cylinder.

STEP 29 | Stand your skew on its edge and transfer the tenon shoulder location from the mark on the tool rest to the turning blank.

STEP 30 | With a spindle gouge, hollow out the tenon so that the smallest diameter of the tenon is ⅝".

STEP 31 | Use calipers to check the diameter.

STEP 32 | With a chisel laid bevel-side down, square up the outside diameter of the tenon.

STEP 33 | Roll the tip of your skew around the end of the tenon to create a small taper, which will help the tenon slide into its mortise.

STEP 34 | Then, with your roughing gouge, cut a taper that runs from a slight shoulder at the tenon to the halfway point along the length of the rung.

STEP 35 | Skew plane the surface of the rung.

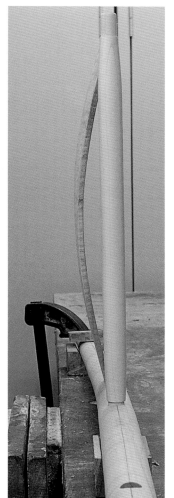

STEP 36 | This photo illustrates two important characteristics of this chair. First, notice the backward curve in the back post. Second, notice the slight difference in entry angle of the back rung and the back slat. As you already saw, the back-rung mortise is centered on the line you created in step 13. Because of its bend, the back slat enters the post at a different angle, with its front surface flush with the line you created in step 13. As you're working on the slat mortises, stop from time to time and test the angle of your mortises by placing a slat in this position and sighting — from the end of the post, as shown here — the relationship between the slat's angle of entry and the rung's angle of entry.

STEP 37 | With a sharp knife and a straightedge, mark the limits of the back slat.

STEP 38 | Although you can create the entire mortise with your mortise chisel, I find it's a bit easier if I first crumb out some of the waste with a $^{3}/_{16}$" drill bit, being careful to observe the correct entry angle.

STEP 39 | Notice that the slat is a little wider than the mortise. This allows you extra material to plane from the width of the slat in order to achieve a tight fit.

STEP 40 | Begin the mortise by tapping the point of your chisel into the scored lines that mark the thickness of the slat.

STEP 41 | With your chisel at a steeper angle, begin to define the side walls of your mortise.

STEP 42 | With your ¼" mortising chisel (ground a bit narrower than that to allow easier access to the ¼" mortise), begin to chip out the waste.

STEP 43 | Stop periodically to lever out the crumbs. I use my finger as the fulcrum to avoid damaging the post.

STEP 44 | As soon as you can, fit the slat into the post and check the angle as discussed in step 36.

STEP 45 | The finished mortise should have tight, clean side walls.

STEP 46 | Apply glue to all the mortises and tenons and bring the front ladder together, squeezing the tenons into their mortises with a pipe clamp. Lay the ladder on your bench top to see that all the parts exist in the same plane. Rack the ladder until it lies flats. Stand the ladder on your bench and check to see that it is square by placing a framing square on your bench top and aligning it with the front ladder posts. Rack the ladder until the front posts are perpendicular to your bench top. Set the ladder aside for at least 8 hours to allow the glue to cure.

STEP 47 | Before applying glue, dry fit the back ladder to see that everything comes together nicely, but don't fully seat the tenons, since they may then be impossible to extricate from their mortises.

STEP 48 | Apply glue to all mortises and tenons and squeeze the back ladder together just as you did the front ladder. Then check to see that the ladder is square, which my son, Andy, is doing here.

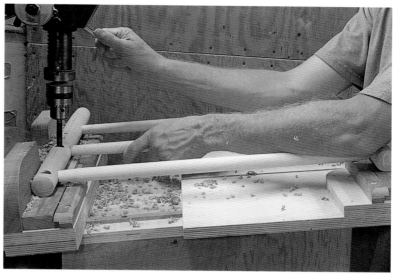

STEP 49 | With a pan of water and a toothbrush, clean up the glue squeeze-out at each joint. Set the ladder aside for at least 8 hours to allow the glue to cure.

STEP 50 | To drill side-rung mortises in the front ladder, position the side-rung mortise jig (SRMJ) so that the table slants away from your body, toward the column on the drill press. Set up the jig so that when the drill bit is extended to its lowest point, it's boring a mortise $^{15}\!/_{16}''$ deep, centered across the width of the post. While it might be possible to establish that setting by measuring, I find it much easier to use trial and error on a scrap of post material turned to the same diameter as the post. Bore mortises in one post. Then reverse the ladder and bore the mortises in the other post.

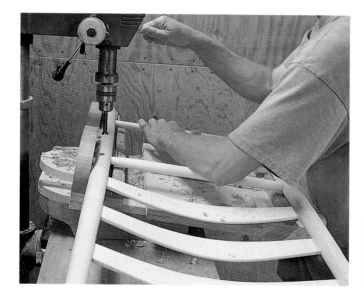

STEP 51 | To drill side-rung mortises in the back ladder, position the SRMJ so that the table slants toward your body, away from the column on the drill press. Once again, set the jig so that when the drill bit is extended to its lowest point, it's boring a mortise $^{15}\!/_{16}''$ deep centered across the width of the post. Bore mortises in one post, then reverse the ladder and bore the mortises in the other post.

STEP 52 | Use a pipe clamp to squeeze the side-rung tenons into their mortises just as you did with the front and back ladders. Wash away glue squeeze-out with water and a toothbrush. Then set the chair aside for at least 8 hours to allow the glue to cure.

Seat Weaving for the Sewing Impaired

Traditionally, tape seats are held in place with sewn joints. When I discovered this, I thought that my inability to manipulate a needle and thread in any meaningful way might prevent me from seating chairs with Shaker tape. Fortunately, however, I discovered an alternate approach, one suitable for the sewing impaired.

STEP 1 | Before you begin to weave a seat with Shaker tape, all the chair's finishing must be completed. In the case of this particular chair, I dyed the wood and finished it with two coats of finish. I then brought it into my house for the actual weaving, and unless your shop is much cleaner than mine, I would recommend you do the same because the weaving process involves having loose coils of tape draped over your bench and onto the floor where they become dust magnets. Those loops of tape that pass over the front and back rungs are called the warp. Those that pass over the side rungs are called the weave. The warp is applied first. Begin by marking locations on the front rungs 90° from the inside face of the two back posts. These two marks divide the area enclosed by the seat rungs into a rectangle and, on each side of that rectangle, a right triangle. Start the warp by stapling (¼" staples) one end of your tape to the inside bottom of the back seat rung against the inside face of the back post. Then wrap the warp strand over the back seat rung and over the front seat rung (just inside one of the marks — the one on the same side of the chair as the back post against which you began).

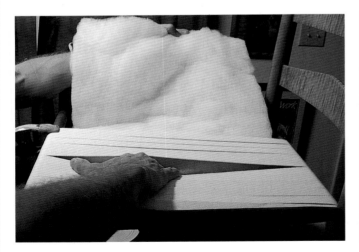

STEP 2 | After you've wrapped your warp strands around the central rectangle of the seat, feed a 1"-thick piece of batting or foam into the gap between the upper and lower layers of the warp. This material should be cut so that it fills the entire area enclosed by the seat rungs. Although the batting may add marginally to the seat's comfort, it has a different purpose: The batting allows the woven seat to maintain a tight appearance if the Shaker tape stretches after weaving.

STEP 3 | Staple the loose end of the tape to the inside bottom of the front seat rung.

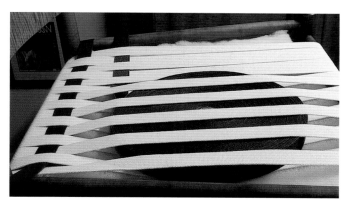

STEP 4 | Begin the weave by stapling one end of your weaver to the bottom inside of one of the two side seat rungs just ahead of the back post.

STEP 5 | The first weave strand alternately passes over one warp strand, then under one warp strand. The second weave strand does the opposite. Early on in the weaving process, the warp strands will be loose enough to pass an entire coil of tape through the warp strands.

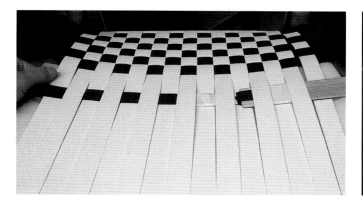

STEP 6 | As you proceed toward the front of the chair, however, the tightness in the warp strands accumulates and the coil will no longer fit through the warp strands. At this point, I switch to my weaving needle, made from a piece of $^3/_{16}$" oak with an eye cut in one end, through which the lead end of my weaver is passed and fastened with tape.

STEP 7 | The gusset strands — those warp strands that fill in the triangles on each side of the central rectangle — can be fit at any time. Each end is fastened in place as shown with a single staple passing through the tape into the inside face of the side seat rung. The other end of each gusset strand is then stapled, from the bottom, on the inside face of the same rung.

STEP 8 | The checkerboard effect is achieved by using different colors for the warp and weave.

3

union village rocker

I was struck by this rocker the moment I saw it in Charles Muller and Tim Rieman's book *The Shaker Chair*, first because it was a distinctive form produced in an Ohio community (my home state), and later, and even more, because of its eccentricity. This is the product of a designer who wasn't afraid to experiment with the post-and-rung form. Notice the distinctive serpentine arms and the little curlicue on the nose of each rocker. These are details not to be found on a Mount Lebanon chair. Add to that the unusual number of slats and the fact that the slats represent several very different shapes, and the result is a chair unlike any other in the world of Shaker chairmaking.

So, very early on in the planning of this book, I decided to include this rocker in my list of projects. On a trip from Cincinnati to our home in Lancaster, Ohio, my wife and I stopped at the Warren County Historical Society's museum in Lebanon, Ohio, so I could take a quick look at the original.

It was all that I hoped it would be, so I made arrangements to return in order to make a measured drawing.

(Please review the previous chapter before starting on this chair.)

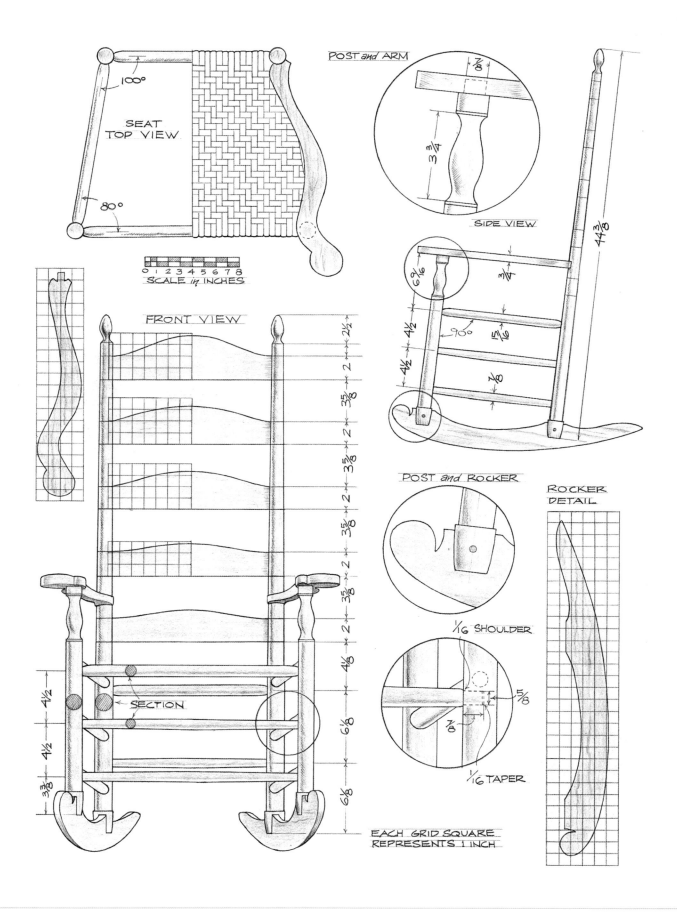

SEAT
TOP VIEW

100°

80°

0 1 2 3 4 5 6 7 8
SCALE in INCHES

POST and ARM

7/8

3 3/4

SIDE VIEW

44 3/8

FRONT VIEW

6 9/16

3/4

90°

15/16

4 1/2   4 1/2

7/8

2 1/2
2
3 3/8
2
3 3/8
2
3 3/8
2
3 3/8
2
4 5/8

4 1/2

4 1/2

3 3/8

SECTION

POST and ROCKER

ROCKER
DETAIL

1/16 SHOULDER

5/8

7/8

1/16 TAPER

6 5/8

6 5/8

EACH GRID SQUARE
REPRESENTS 1 INCH

inches (millimeters)

QUANTITY	PART	STOCK	THICKNESS	(mm)	WIDTH	(mm)	LENGTH	(mm)	COMMENTS
2	back posts	curly maple	1¹¹⁄₁₆ dia.	(43)			44³⁄₈	(1128)	
2	front posts	curly maple	1¹¹⁄₁₆ dia.	(43)			20¹⁄₈	(511)	This length includes a ⁵⁄₈" dia. × ⁵⁄₈" (16mm dia. × 16mm) tenon that fits into a mortise cut in the underside of the arm.
3	front rungs	curly maple	⁷⁄₈ dia.	(22)			19¹³⁄₁₆	(504)	
2	back rungs	curly maple	⁷⁄₈ dia.	(22)			14³⁄₄	(375)	
6	side rungs	curly maple	⁷⁄₈ dia.	(22)			15¹⁄₄	(387)	
2	arms	curly maple	³⁄₄	(19)	3⁷⁄₁₆	(87)	19³⁄₈	(493)	This length includes a ¹⁄₂" dia. × ⁷⁄₈" (13mm dia. × 22mm) tenon on one end.
1	top slat	curly maple	¹⁄₄	(6)	3³⁄₄	(95)	14⁵⁄₁₆	(364)	This length includes a ⁷⁄₁₆" (11mm) tenon on each end.
1	upper middle slat	curly maple	¹⁄₄	(6)	3¹⁄₄	(82)	14¹⁄₂	(369)	This length includes a ¹⁄₂" (13mm) tenon on each end.
1	middle slat	curly maple	¹⁄₄	(6)	2⁷⁄₈	(73)	14¹³⁄₁₆	(377)	This length includes a ⁵⁄₈" (16mm) tenon on each end.
2	bottom slats	curly maple	¹⁄₄	(5)	2¹¹⁄₁₆	(69)	15¹⁄₈	(384)	This length includes a ³⁄₄" (19mm) tenon on each end.
2	rockers	curly maple	⁹⁄₁₆	(14)	4⁹⁄₁₆	(116)	28⁷⁄₁₆	(722)	
4	rocker dowels	curly maple	¹⁄₄ dia.	(6)			1³⁄₄	(45)	These are trimmed flush after assembly.

NOTE: You'll need the front-rung and side-rung mortise jigs from the previous chapter. Also, the seat requires about two hanks of ¹⁄₂" (13mm) splint, which is available from Connecticut Cane and Reed, as well as other suppliers (see Suppliers at the end of the book).

STEP 2 | Curly maple is notorious for tearing out when it's planed. If the tear-out is relatively shallow, use a butt chisel to level the surface as shown in step 20 of the previous chapter. If the tear-out is deeper — as was the case with this particular set of slats — try a Stanley No. 80.

STEP 1 | This is the original chair in its home at the Warren County Historical Society's museum. It's made of mixed woods: straight-grained maple for the posts, slats and rockers, curly maple for the arms and most likely ash for the rungs.

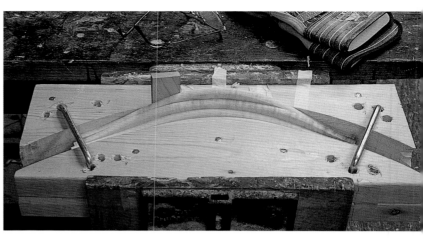

STEP 3 | The slats are rounded on the front side. The rough shaping can be done with a spokeshave, as I'm doing here, or it can be done with a rasp.

STEP 4 | I bent the slats in the same form I used for the slats on the chair in the preceding chapter. Because the extrawide top slat developed a little wrinkle after I took it from the steamer, I tapped a wedge between the slat and the form to keep the slat straight.

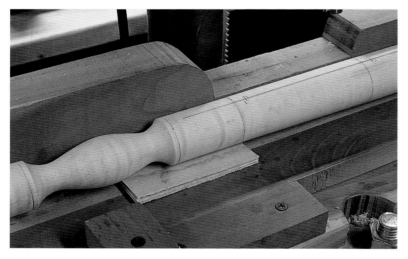

STEP 5 | The front posts are tapered. It is, therefore, necessary to shim underneath their thinner end in order to keep the center lines of the slat mortises 90° from the center lines of the posts. This taper also makes it difficult to find the center of the post with the lead point of the Forstner bit. When drilling the front-rung mortises, set the fence of the front-rung mortise jig so that the bit hits the center of the post at the location of the bottom-rung mortise. As you move up the post, pull the rung away from the fence so that the lead point of the Forstner bit hits the line at each of the other two front-rung mortise locations.

STEP 6 | Assemble the front ladder as shown in step 46 of the previous chapter. I chose to make each of the front rungs all the same length. In order to keep the center lines of the front posts 90° from the center lines of the rungs it was necessary to set the shoulders of the tenons on the middle rung $1/16$" away from the post and the shoulders of the tenons on the seat rung a full $1/8$" from the post. On the original chair, the shoulders are brought tight against the posts, which results in a chair frame where the front posts taper from the rockers to the arms. (This is a complication I decided to avoid, although, now that I look back on it, I think it wouldn't have made much difference.)

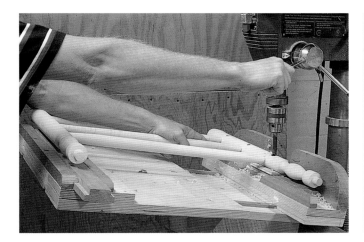

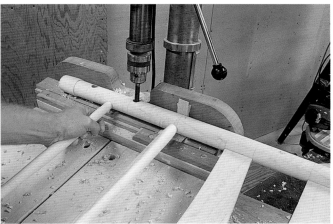

STEP 7 | Because of the front post taper, shim underneath the upper section of the front post when drilling the side-rung mortises. The shims make it possible for the center line of the post to be 90° from the center line of each mortise. As you did in step 5, set the fence of the side-rung mortise jig so that the bit will hit the center of the post at the location of the bottom-rung mortise. Then as you move up the post, pull the rung away from the fence so that the lead point of the Forstner bit hits the line at each of the other two front-rung mortise locations.

STEP 8 | Assemble the back ladder as shown in steps 47 and 48 of the previous chapter. Because of the enlargement at the bottom of each back post, use shims to bring the center line of the post to right angles with the center line of each side-rung mortise. Notice that in this photo I'm using a different method to align the lead point of the Forstner bit with the center line of the post. Instead of pulling the post away from the fence as I move up the post, I've shimmed both underneath and behind the post. This method will also work for the mortises in steps 5 and 7.

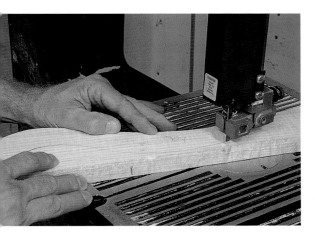

STEP 9 | Cut out the arms on your band saw.

STEP 10 | Shape the tenons at the end of each arm with a paring chisel and a wide-sweep carving gouge. The paring chisel is used to shape the actual tenon. The carving gouge is used to create the curved tenon shoulder that butts up against the chair post. Make sure that the arc of that shoulder is the same as the diameter of the post at the point where the post and shoulder will meet.

STEP 11 | Carefully measure the distance from the post to the center of the mortise on the bottom of each arm (the tenon at the top of each front post will fit into these mortises) and cut those mortises with a $\frac{5}{8}$" Forstner bit.

STEP 12 | Tap the tenons of the side rungs (and arms) into place. Then squeeze the front and back ladders together with a pipe clamp. Don't fully seat a tenon on your first stop at a particular location along the post. Work your way up and down one side of the chair, squeezing each tenon into place $\frac{1}{2}$" at a time until all three on that side are fully seated. Then switch over to the other side of the chair. Wash away the glue squeeze-out with water and a tooth-brush, then set the chair aside for at least 8 hours to allow the glue to cure.

STEP 13 | Cut out the rockers on your band saw. Then remove the band saw marks with a plane on the bottom edges and a spoke-shave or a rasp on the top edges.

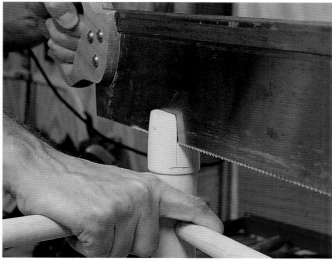

STEP 14 | Carefully lay out the rocker notches at the base of each post. Then define the sidewalls of each notch with a backsaw. Be sure to keep the saw well inside the lines.

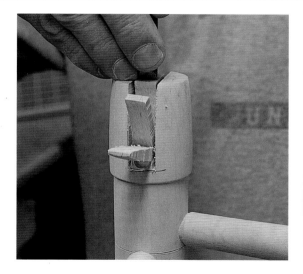

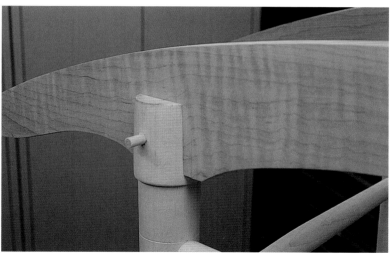

STEP 15 | Drill a hole from the front to the back of the notch just above the base of each notch. The hole can be seen here at the base of the chip closest to the camera. Then break the chips out with a chisel and pare the notch to its final dimensions.

STEP 16 | When the rockers are fit into their notches, drill a ¼" hole that passes through the post and the rocker. Then tap a glued ¼" dowel into that hole. Cut off the ends of the dowel and pare smooth.

STEP 17 | Apply a first coat of finish to the chair. After the finish has dried, begin weaving the seat. Soak the splint in a tub of warm water for an hour or more before beginning the weaving process. This soaking helps to soften the material and makes weaving it much easier. While the splint is soaking, lay out the central rectangle on your seat rungs. Measure the distance between the two back posts just above the back seat rung. Then measure the distance between the two front posts just above the front seat rung. Subtract the back measurement from the front measurement to find the difference, then make a mark on each end of the front seat rung that is one-half of that difference from the front post on one end and one-half of that differ-

ence from the front post on the other end. Lay a blanket on your bench top to protect your chair arms from being scratched during the seat weaving process. Remove one hank from the water. Open it and pull out one of the longest strips of splint. One side of each strip is smoother than the other. The smoother side should be used as the seat side. Begin by taping one end of a long strip to the back of a side seat rung as shown. Then begin to wrap these strips, known as the warp, around the front seat rung (just to the right of the mark you just made on the front seat rung) and the back seat rung. When you reach the end of the strip, clamp it to the back seat rung.

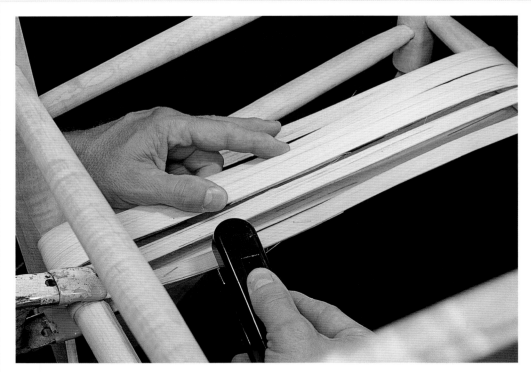

STEP 18 | Pull out another long strip of splint. Invert the chair so that it is lying upside down on your bench. Lay 6" or 8" of that new strip over the end of the old strip and fasten the two together with three staples. (These joints should all be made on the bottom side of the seat.)

STEP 19 | This is what the seat should look like from its bottom side (inverted on your bench) when you have completed filling in the area between the two back posts.

STEP 20 | Start the first weaver on the bottom side of the seat. The pattern for this particular weave is under two strands of warp and over two strands of warp.

STEP 21 | Wrap your weaver around the side seat rung and continue across the top side of the seat. Notice the short weaver that fills in the space between the back posts. Its ends are simply tucked under. Notice, too, that the first full-length weaver (which you brought around from the bottom) enters the warp strand one row past the entry point of the short weaver.

STEP 22 | A new length of weaver is joined by lapping it 6" or 8" over the end of the previous weaver. The tightness of the weave and the warp will hold the joint in place.

STEP 23 | Fill in the gussets — those triangular areas to the left and right of the main rectangle of warp — as shown. Weave them back into the weavers, tucking the ends underneath. Weave the other ends into the weavers on the bottom side of the seat. After the seat has been woven and the splint has dried, apply a second coat of finish to the chair and a first coat to the seat.

transitional rocker

Strictly speaking, this isn't a Shaker reproduction. In the 15 or so years I've been building this chair, I've tinkered with back post alignment, front post turnings, arm shape and the transition from back post to cushion rail. But it did begin as a reproduction of a specific Shaker original, and it is an assembly of clearly Shaker details.

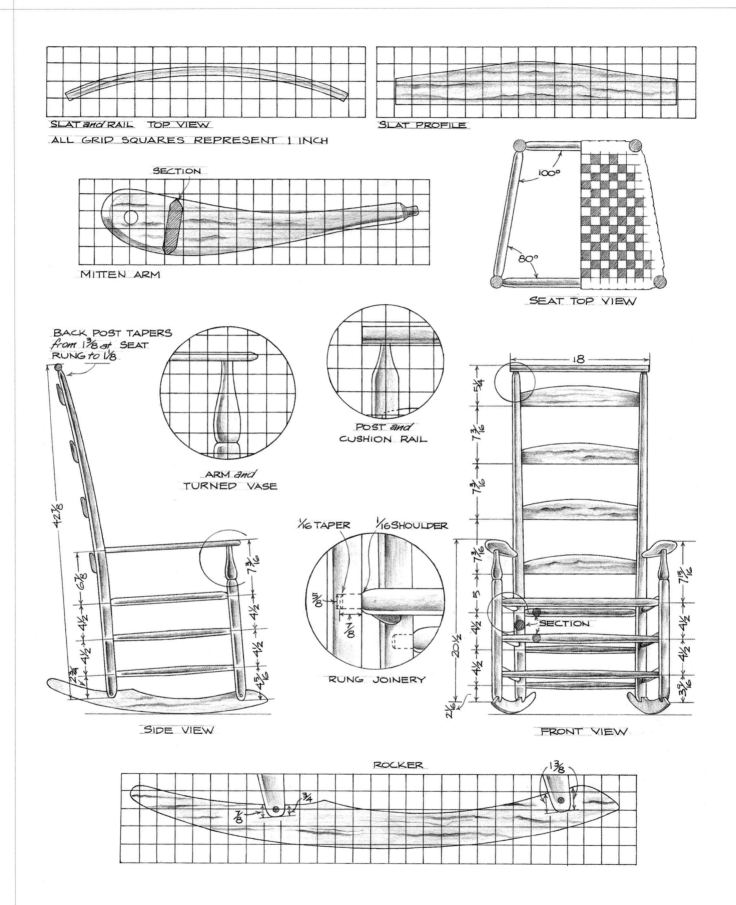

SLAT *and* RAIL TOP VIEW

SLAT PROFILE

ALL GRID SQUARES REPRESENT 1 INCH

SECTION

MITTEN ARM

100°

80°

SEAT TOP VIEW

BACK POST TAPERS
from 1 3/8 *at* SEAT
RUNG *to* 1/8

ARM *and*
TURNED VASE

POST *and*
CUSHION RAIL

42 7/8

6 7/8

4 1/2

4 1/2

4 1/2

4 1/2

4 5/16

2 3/4

7 3/16

SIDE VIEW

1/16 TAPER   1/16 SHOULDER

11/8

7/8

RUNG JOINERY

18

5 1/4

7 3/16

7 3/16

7 3/16

5

4 1/2

20 1/2

4 1/2

2 1/16

7 15/16

4 1/2

3 3/16

SECTION

FRONT VIEW

ROCKER

1 3/8

3/4

7/8

inches (millimeters)

QUANTITY	PART	STOCK	THICKNESS	(mm)	WIDTH	(mm)	LENGTH	(mm)	COMMENTS
2	front posts	hard maple	1³/₈ dia.	(35)			20⁹/₁₆	(522)	This includes a ¹³/₁₆" (21mm) tenon on the top of the post, ³/₄" (19mm) of which passes through the arm. The remaining ¹/₁₆" (2mm) is pared flush with the surface of the arm.
2	back posts	hard maple	³/₈ dia.	(10)			42⁷/₈	(1089)	Tenons at the tops of the back posts should be made ¹/₈" (3mm) longer so they can be pared flush with the outside diameter of the cushion rail.
3	front rungs	hard maple	⁷/₈ dia.	(22)			21¹/₄	(539)	This includes a ⁷/₈" (22mm) tenon on each end.
6	side rungs	hard maple	⁷/₈ dia.	(22)			16¹/₂	(419)	This includes a ⁷/₈" (22mm) tenon on each end.
3	back rungs	hard maple	³/₈ dia.	(10)			15¹/₂	(394)	This includes a ⁷/₈" (22mm) tenon on each end.
1	top slat	hard maple	¹/₄	(6)	2¹/₂	(64)	16¹/₂	(419)	This includes a ¹/₂" (13mm) tenon on each end.
1	upper middle slat	hard maple	¹/₄.	(6)	2¹/₂	(64)	16¹/₄	(412)	This includes a ⁵/₈" (16mm) tenon on each end.
1	lower middle slat	hard maple	¹/₄	(6)	2¹/₂	(64)	16¹/₄	(412)	This includes a ¹¹/₁₆" (18mm) tenon on each end.
1	bottom slat	hard maple	¹/₄	(6)	2¹/₂	(64)	16	(406)	This includes a ³/₄" (19mm) tenon on each end.
2	arms	hard maple	³/₄	(19)	3¹/₂	(89)	18	(457)	
4	wedges	hard maple							Cut to fit notches in tops of posts.
2	rockers	hard maple	³/₈	(10)	3³/₄	(95)	28	(711)	
4	rocker pegs	hard maple	¹/₄ dia.	(6)			1⁷/₁₆	(36)	
1	cushion rail	hard maple	³/₄ dia.	(19)			18	(457)	

STEP 1 | The back posts terminate in a ⁵/₁₆" tenon that passes through the cushion rail. However, turning one end of such a long post to such a small diameter is very tricky, so stop at a more robust ⁷/₁₆", then remove the posts from the lathe, assemble the chair, and just before installing the cushion rail use hand tools to reduce the tenon to its finished ⁵/₁₆" diameter. (Be sure to use your off hand or another steady rest when turning the ⁷/₁₆"-diameter section at the top of the post.) This photo of a pair of back posts locked into the bending form shows the oversize diameter of the tenons that will later pass through the cushion rail.

STEP 2 | Before gluing up the ladders, dry assemble them to check the fit of all the tenons, but don't fully seat any at this stage.

STEP 3 | The arms are shaped with a drawknife and spokeshave. This is hard work when you're using dry lumber, but with a bit of determination, it is possible. Notice the reference line drawn around the edge of the arms about a third of the way up from the bottom. The crowned bevel around the top of the finished arm and the crowned bevel on the bottom of the finished arm will meet at the line.

STEP 4 | Use a pair of puppets on a pipe clamp, which is held in a vise, to raise the arm high enough to work it without breaking your knuckles on your bench. The puppet on the head-clamp end has a $\frac{3}{4}$"-diameter hole bored about $\frac{1}{2}$" deep to accept the roughed-in tenon and one end of the arm. The inside surface of the other puppet has been dished with a carving tool to accept the nose of the arm.

STEP 5 | Please see the preceding chapters for information about assembling the body of the chair. Once the frame has been assembled, install the arms. Each is held in place with a tenon on the back-post end and a mortise through which the tenon at the top of the front post has been wedged. Lay out the notches for the wedges by laying a straightedge across the tops of both posts parallel with the front rungs. Then mark the center of each post along the edge of the straightedge. The notches, which should be about $\frac{1}{8}$" wide at the top of the tenon, are laid out around this line. Then drill a $\frac{1}{8}$" hole through the tenon at the base of the tenon. This hole will reduce the chances of a split spreading from the notch down into the post.

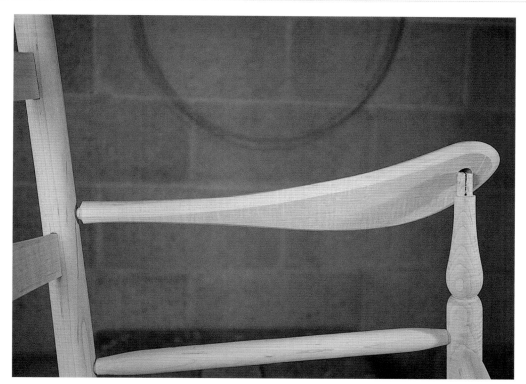

STEP 6 | To install the arm, push the tenon on the back post end into its mortise with the arm standing on its edge as shown. Rotate the arm so that mortise near the nose of the arm passes over the tenon at the top of the front post. Then tap the wedge, which should be very slightly wider than the $\frac{5}{8}$"-diameter tenon, into the notch. Cut off the wedge surplus. Then pare and sand both the wedge and tenon flat.

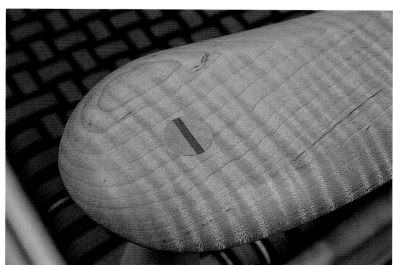

STEP 7 | This is how the wedged through-tenon should look after the wedge has been cut off and pared flat.

STEP 8 | This is the finished wedged through-tenon at the top of one of the back posts. Notice that the wedge is placed perpendicular to the grain direction of the cushion rail. This is important because aligning the wedge with the grain direction of the cushion rail could result in splitting the rail.

bentwood boxes and carriers

No book about Shaker woodworking would be complete without mention of the quintessential Shaker-made objects: oval boxes and carriers.

The seven pieces described in this chapter were taken from measured drawings in John Kassay's *The Book of Shaker Furniture* and one of Ejner Handberg's books of drawings. The exception is the large carrier. That piece was made by scaling up the handle from a smaller piece in Handberg's book and attaching it to the body of the largest oval box in the series shown here.

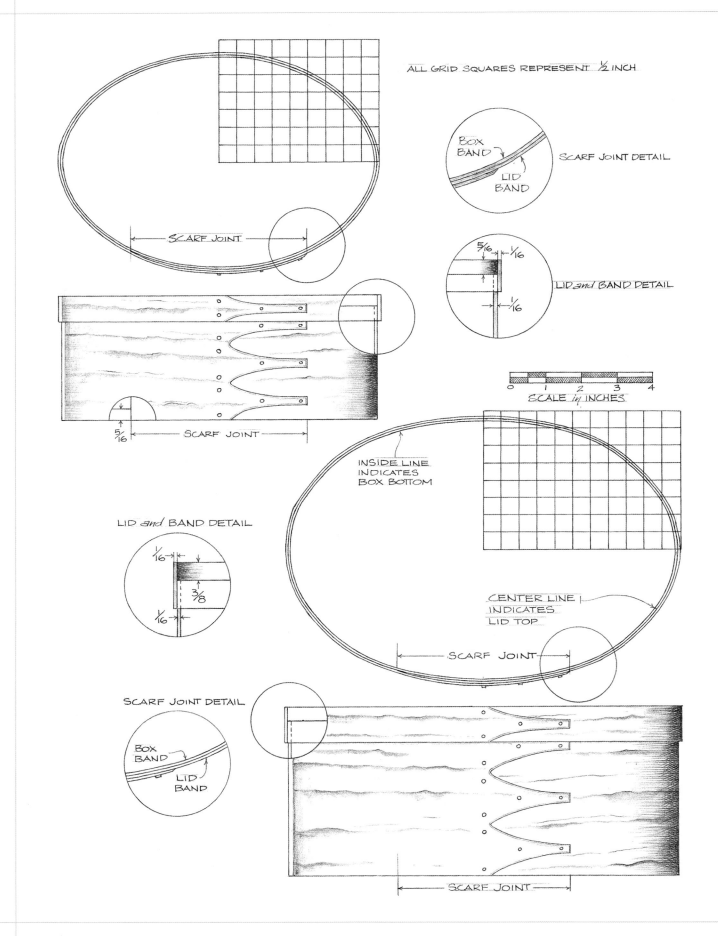

ALL GRID SQUARES REPRESENT ½ INCH

SCARF JOINT DETAIL

BOX BAND

LID BAND

LID and BAND DETAIL

5/16   1/16

1/16

SCARF JOINT

SCARF JOINT

5/16

SCALE in INCHES

0   1   2   3   4

INSIDE LINE INDICATES BOX BOTTOM

LID and BAND DETAIL

1/16

3/8

1/16

CENTER LINE INDICATES LID TOP

SCARF JOINT

SCARF JOINT DETAIL

BOX BAND

LID BAND

SCARF JOINT

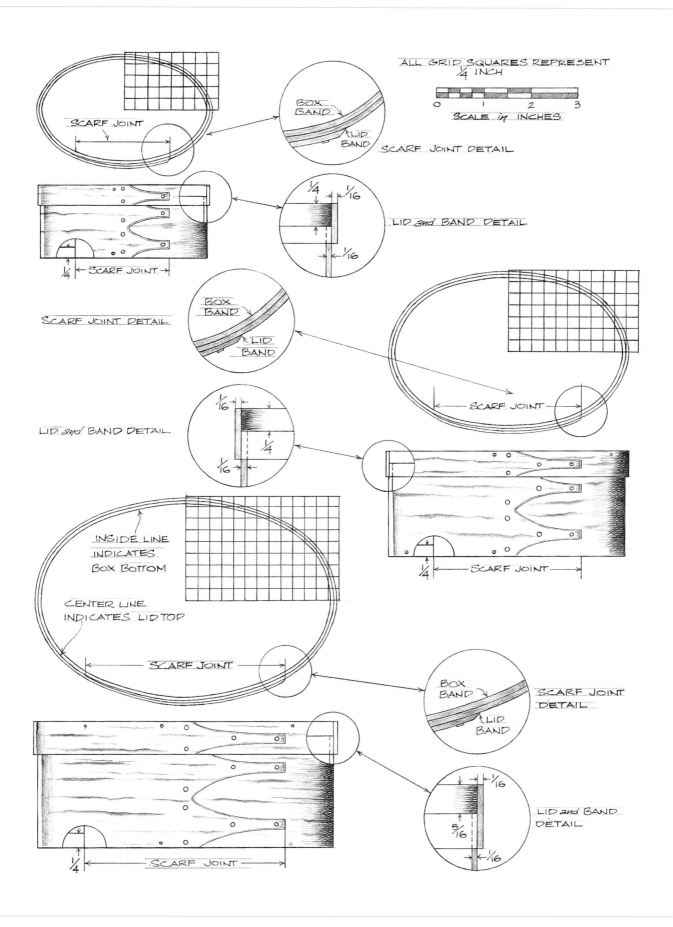

ALL GRID SQUARES REPRESENT
¼ INCH

0   1   2   3
SCALE IN INCHES

SCARF JOINT

BOX
BAND

LID
BAND

SCARF JOINT DETAIL

SCARF JOINT

¼
SCARF JOINT

¼   1/16

1/16

LID and BAND DETAIL

SCARF JOINT DETAIL

BOX
BAND

LID
BAND

SCARF JOINT

1/16

¼

1/16

LID and BAND DETAIL

¼
SCARF JOINT

INSIDE LINE
INDICATES
BOX BOTTOM

CENTER LINE
INDICATES LID TOP

SCARF JOINT

BOX
BAND

LID
BAND

SCARF JOINT
DETAIL

¼
SCARF JOINT

1/16

5/16

1/16

LID and BAND
DETAIL

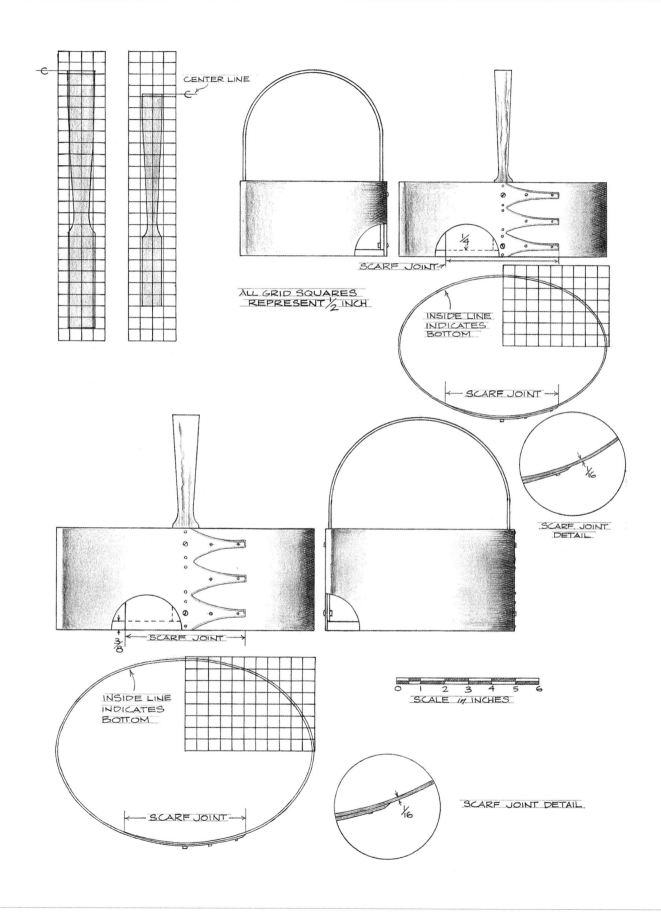

C
C

CENTER LINE

C

ALL GRID SQUARES
REPRESENT ½ INCH

SCARF JOINT

¼

INSIDE LINE
INDICATES
BOTTOM

SCARF JOINT

SCARF JOINT
DETAIL

⅟16

⅜

SCARF JOINT

INSIDE LINE
INDICATES
BOTTOM

SCARF JOINT

SCARF JOINT DETAIL

⅟16

0 1 2 3 4 5 6
SCALE *in* INCHES

NOTE: I have used a combination of cherry and maple for these boxes, with ash for the handles, but you can use whatever wood you prefer or have handy.

LARGEST BOX AND CARRIER • inches (millimeters)

QUANTITY	PART	STOCK	THICKNESS	(mm)	WIDTH	(mm)	LENGTH	(mm)	COMMENTS
1	box band		$^1/_{16}$	(2)	$4^7/_{16}$	(113)	$35^3/_8$	(899)	
1	bottom		$^3/_8$	(10)	$7^3/_8$	(188)	$10^5/_8$	(270)	
1	lid band		$^1/_{16}$	(2)	1	(25)	36	(914)	used if making the box
1	top		$^3/_8$	(10)	$7^1/_2$	(191)	$10^3/_4$	(273)	used if making the box
1	carrier handle		$^1/_8$	(3)	$1^1/_8$	(28)	$22^1/_4$	(565)	used if making the carrier

SECOND LARGEST BOX AND CARRIER • inches (millimeters)

QUANTITY	PART	STOCK	THICKNESS	(mm)	WIDTH	(mm)	LENGTH	(mm)	COMMENTS
1	box band		$^1/_{16}$	(2)	$3^1/_4$	(82)	$28^1/_2$	(724)	
1	bottom		$^5/_{16}$	(8)	6	(152)	$8^3/_4$	(222)	
1	lid band		$^1/_{16}$	(2)	$^3/_4$	(19)	$28^5/_8$	(727)	used if making the box
1	top		$^5/_{16}$	(8)	$6^1/_8$	(155)	$8^7/_8$	(225)	used if making the box
1	carrier handle		$^1/_8$	(3)	$^3/_4$	(19)	$18^1/_4$	(463)	used if making the carrier

THIRD LARGEST BOX AND CARRIER • inches (millimeters)

QUANTITY	PART	STOCK	THICKNESS	(mm)	WIDTH	(mm)	LENGTH	(mm)	COMMENTS
1	box band		$^1/_{16}$	(2)	$2^3/_8$	(61)	21	(533)	
1	bottom		$^5/_{16}$	(8)	$4^1/_8$	(105)	$6^1/_8$	(155)	
1	lid band		$^1/_{16}$	(2)	$^{11}/_{16}$	(18)	$21^1/_8$	(536)	
1	top		$^5/_{16}$	(8)	$4^1/_4$	(108)	$6^1/_4$	(158)	

FOURTH LARGEST BOX AND CARRIER • inches (millimeters)

QUANTITY	PART	STOCK	THICKNESS	(mm)	WIDTH	(mm)	LENGTH	(mm)	COMMENTS
1	box band		1/16	(2)	2	(51)	17 1/2	(445)	
1	bottom		1/4	(6)	3 3/16	(81)	4 3/4	(121)	
1	lid band		1/16	(2)	9/16	(14)	17 3/8	(442)	
1	top		1/4	(6)	2 5/16	(59)	4 7/8	(124)	

SMALLEST BOX AND CARRIER • inches (millimeters)

QUANTITY	PART	STOCK	THICKNESS	(mm)	WIDTH	(mm)	LENGTH	(mm)	COMMENTS
1	box band		1/16	(2)	1 3/8	(35)	12	(305)	
1	bottom		1/4	(6)	2 1/4	(57)	3 1/2	(89)	
1	lid band		1/16	(2)	1/2	(13)	12	(305)	
1	top		1/4	(6)	2 3/8	(61)	3 3/8	(86)	

NOTES: These boxes and carriers can all be made from 36" (914mm) sheets of 1/16" (2mm) veneer sold by Constantines. These sheets are available in several different species. The No. 1 copper tacks used to fasten these boxes can be purchased from Woodcraft. The carrier handles are traditionally attached with copper tacks. I opted for what I see as the cleaner look of small brass bolts and nuts. Information for all the suppliers listed can be found in the back of the book.

hardware and supplies

1/2" (13mm) brads or wooden pegs

STEP 1 | Before you can make boxes, you must make molds. Molds for the smaller boxes can be band-sawn from scrap; however, the molds for the larger forms will likely need to be glued up. The mold for the largest box and carrier in this chapter was glued up from some 6/4 maple too unsightly to use as chair posts.

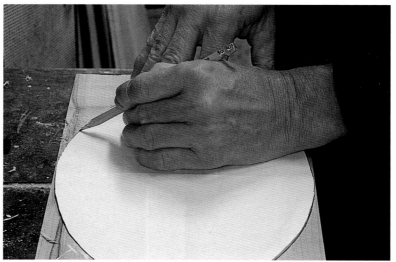

STEP 2 | I create my oval patterns freehand. I begin by penciling a center line on my paper. I mark the greatest width and length on this paper. I then sketch in a half oval that just meets these limits. Next, I fold the paper, creasing it along the center line, and trace the second half from the first half. This produces a bilaterally symmetrical oval. Trace the pattern on the mold stock.

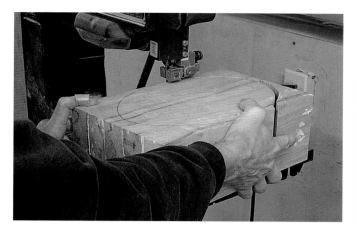

STEP 3 | Cut out the mold on your band saw.

STEP 4 | Use a block plane to remove saw marks. (The lid mold is made the same way.)

STEP 5 | Oval boxes and baskets are held together with tiny brass tacks driven through the box bands and peened against a hard metal surface. Some boxmakers use all wood molds, peening the tacks on a separate round anvil made from a piece of steel pipe. I use a different method. I cement a piece of scrap metal into a shallow mortise in each box and lid mold, peening the tacks against that metal while the bands are still on the molds. The metal shown here was taken from a cement trowel I bought for a quarter at a flea market. I cut out an appropriately sized rectangle of metal, then worked it until it had taken the curvature of that section of the mold into which it would be fastened. (Be sure to cement the metal to that section of the mold over which the fingers will be tacked. The line of tacks to the right of the fingers should be placed at the halfway point along the length of the box.)

STEP 6 | Use contact cement to fasten the metal into place.

STEP 7 | Rip the veneer to width with a utility knife guided by a straightedge. The veneer can be used full thickness for all but the smallest of the two boxes. For these boxes, the thickness must be reduced using either a block plane or a scraper. The smallest should be made of material about $1/32$" in thickness. The next smallest, about $3/64$". (I blush when I note these very precise-sounding measurements, because I've never actually measured the thickness of these bands. I just plane and scrape until I get the material somewhere in the ballpark.)

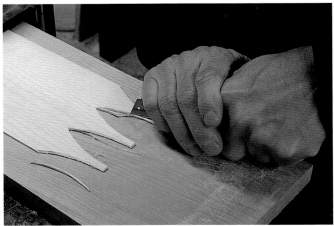

STEP 8 | After tracing the fingers onto the box and lid bands, cut out the fingers on your band saw, using a fine-tooth blade.

STEP 9 | With the utility knife, cut the bevels on each finger. Use a paring chisel to cut the bevel at the end of each finger. Touch up the bevels with a bit of 150-grit sandpaper.

STEP 10 | With a block plane, feather the square ends of the box and lid bands so that they taper from $\frac{1}{16}$" thickness to 0" thickness. This taper should extend to that part of the band that laps under the fingers. This taper eliminates the unsightly bulge that occurs when stiff $\frac{1}{16}$" material at the end of the band presses against the inside of the boxes and lids.

STEP 11 | Soak the box and lid bands in warm (or hot) water for 20 to 30 minutes to soften them before bending. Then wrap the bands around the molds and secure them with rubber bands. Notice the flexible caul covering the fingers. This is made from narrow strips of wood held together with duct tape. Although I know of no one else who uses this caul, I find it simplifies the process of wrapping the bands. Without the caul, splits can run out between the fingers. I'd like to say a word here about soaking bands. Some makers insist on 180° water, while some say 200° water. My experience is that water temperature doesn't make much difference. I've done box-making demonstrations for woodworking groups using cold tap water. And once, just to be contrary, I used ice water, which worked just fine. My recommendation? If you have a source of warm water, use it. If you don't, don't worry about it. Allow the bands to dry for a couple of days before removing the caul and driving the tacks.

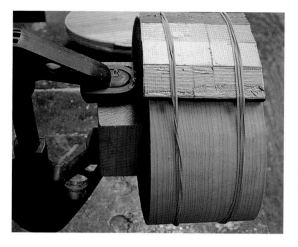

STEP 12 | I've screwed a block of scrap to the bottom of each mold, which allows me to hold the mold in a bar clamp, which is, itself, clamped in a vise. This presents the mold at a convenient working height.

STEP 13 | Mark the tack locations along lines made with your try square. Then predrill the tack holes with a wire bit. Bit size is important. It should be great enough to permit the tacks to be driven without splitting fingers, but it should be small enough to allow a snug fit of the tack body in the hole. Experiment on scraps of veneer until you find the correct bit size.

STEP 14 | After you've tacked the box body together, carefully hold the body against your bottom stock. Trace the interior of the box on that stock. Then, before moving to the band saw, take a moment to study the bottom shape. Sometimes the bending process will result in a slightly misshapen box body. With your pencil, correct any oddities in bottom disc shape, then cut the bottom disc on your band saw, being careful to stay about $1/32$" outside the line.

STEP 15 | With a disc sander, clean up the band saw marks on the bottom disc. Make frequent checks of the disc fit in the box body. The goal is to arrive at a perfect fit at the same moment you arrive at a perfectly oval disc shape.

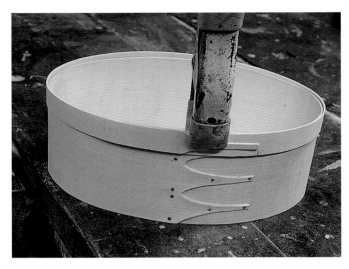

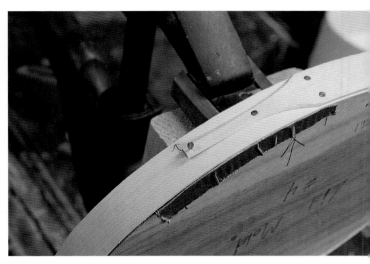

STEP 16 | Fit the lid band for the boxes snugly around the box body. Mark the lap as shown here.

STEP 17 | Tack the lid band together.

STEP 18 | Pop the bottom disc out. Tape the lid band to the box band so that the lid and box fingers align correctly. Then invert the box on the lid material and mark the lid disc. Cut and fit as you did with the box bottom.

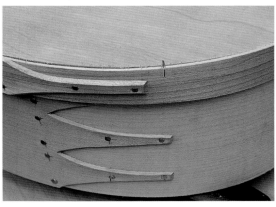

STEP 19 | Fit the lid disc just as you did the bottom disc. It's unlikely that the lid finger will align perfectly with the box fingers your first time out, so mark the correct lid/finger location on the lid disc as I've done here. Then pop the disc out and reinsert it so that the finger aligns with the mark.

STEP 20 | Purists may object because I use ½" brads to fasten the lid and bottom discs. It's true that most Shaker boxes used wooden pegs for this operation, and I have used wooden pegs, but I like the convenience of brads. Whether you use pegs or brads, you must first drill to avoid splitting the lid and box material.

STEP 21 | The handles for the carriers must be thicknessed and shaped before they can be bent.

STEP 22 | The handles are steamed for 30 minutes (see project two, step 21 for a look at my steamer.). They are then brought into the shop and bent around the handle forms as shown here. Although I've done this by myself, this is a job best done by three people: one to remove the handle from the steamer and reestablish the other handles in the steamer, another to carry the handle (quickly) to the form and enact the bend, and one other person to position the clamp. The larger handles are bent from ash, which is nearly idiotproof. But the smaller handles are made from hard maple, which, although it bends well, is not idiotproof. Particularly when bending them from maple, you must flex that part of the handle that will be bent between your hands to limber it before you position the handle on the form.

STEP 23 | As much as possible, you should work to create pleasurable moments in your shop. For me, gluing up a chair frame is one such moment. Another is sanding a run of oval boxes.

tripod table

The first half dozen Shaker tripod tables I made had hand-cut sliding dovetails. I enjoyed the process of cutting those elegant joints, but they were very time-consuming. Then, maybe 10 years ago, I saw a magazine article about the construction of an 18th-century Chippendale tripod table, and the author of the article was attaching the legs to the pedestal with simple tenons, not sliding dovetails.

That article was a revelation. Tenons just made good sense, particularly when I con-sidered that nearly all the tripod tables I had made were made of cherry, which is probably the most fragile hardwood I use in my shop. I know that the holding power of the table's joinery was almost entirely attributable to the glue. The mechanical advantage of the dovetail over the tenon in this particular application was so slight as to be insignificant. I was certain, for example, that it would take little stress on a dry joint to break the dovetail out of its housing in the base of the pedestal.

So why bother with a dovetail?

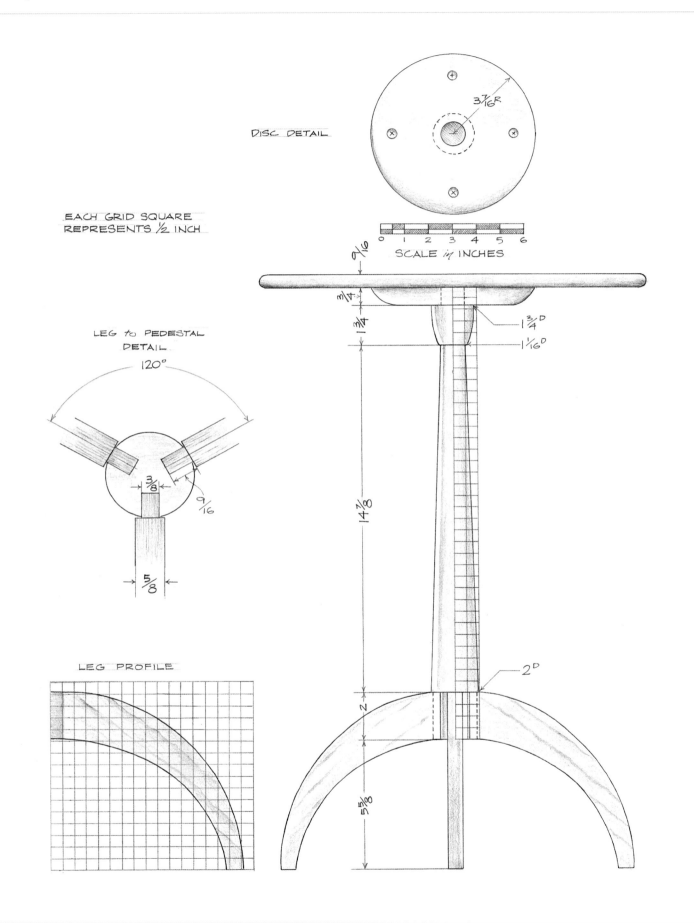

DISC DETAIL

$3\frac{7}{16}R$

EACH GRID SQUARE
REPRESENTS ½ INCH

SCALE in INCHES

LEG to PEDESTAL
DETAIL

120°

$\frac{3}{8}$

$\frac{9}{16}$

$\frac{5}{8}$

LEG PROFILE

$\frac{9}{16}$

$\frac{3}{4}$

$1\frac{3}{4}$

$1\frac{3}{4}^D$

$1\frac{1}{16}^D$

$14\frac{7}{8}$

2^D

2

$5\frac{5}{8}$

inches (millimeters)

QUANTITY	PART	STOCK	THICKNESS	(mm)	WIDTH	(mm)	LENGTH	(mm)	COMMENTS
1	tabletop	cherry	$9/16$	(14)	$16^1/4$ dia.	(412)			
1	support disc	cherry	$3/4$	(19)	$6^7/8$ dia.	(174)			The top is fastened to the support disc with four No. 8 × 1" (25mm) wood screws.
1	pedestal	cherry	2 dia.	(51)			$19^3/8$	(493)	
3	legs	cherry	$5/8$	(16)	$4^1/16$	(104)	$11^3/16$	(284)	
1	sheet-metal disc	cherry	$1^3/4$ dia.	(45)					The sheet-metal disc is fastened to the bottoms of the legs with three No. 6 × $3/4$" (19mm) wood screws.

STEP 1 | With your roughing gouge, reduce the pedestal blank to a cylinder. Then mark the various divisions along its length. The measurements shown here indicate the diameters at the marked locations.

STEP 2 | With a roughing gouge and a butt chisel laid bevel-side down on your rest, create the tenon at the top of the pedestal. (This process is illustrated in steps 30 through 32 of project two.) The butt chisel alone can create the base against which the legs will be fit. Then use a parting tool to set the diameter of the post where it meets the bottom of the cup.

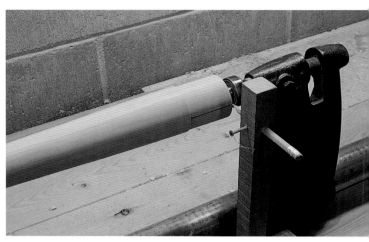

STEP 3 | The cup can be shaped with the skew used as a plane, or laid flat and used as a scraper. Use a fingernail gouge to shape the long taper below the cup.

STEP 4 | After you've sanded the pedestal, mark three equally spaced lines around the circumference of the base. These lines mark the centers of the three mortises you'll cut for the leg tenons. (The process of using the lathe's indexing head to divide the circumference of spindles is described in steps 12 and 13 of project two.)

STEP 5 | Make three marks 120° apart, each of which bisects the space between the lines. You'll use these lines to mark the centers of each mortise on the pedestal's end grain.

STEP 6 | Fix the pedestal on your bench with a pair of U-blocks and a clamp.

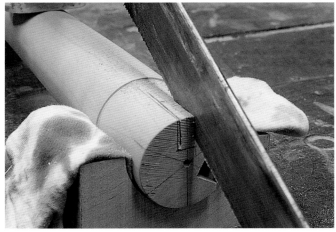

STEP 7 | Mark the limits of each mortise, using the lines you drew on the lathe as your guide. Take a few minutes to study this photo. Notice that the center line mark on the end grain of each mortise is made by connecting the mortise's center line and the line that marks the division between the table's other two mortises on the opposite side of the spindle.

STEP 8 | Rough in the sides of each mortise with a backsaw.

STEP 9 | Begin chopping out the waste with a mortise chisel.

STEP 10 | Use a paring chisel to work up to the lines.

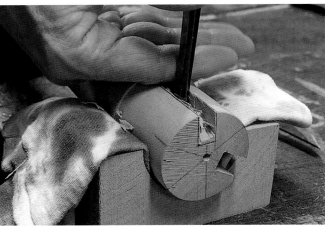

STEP 11 | The mortise chisel can be used as shown here to create the flat at the bottom of the mortise.

STEP 12 | Use a knife against a straightedge (I'm using an old flexible scraper) clamped to the work to mark the shoulders of each tenon.

STEP 13 | With a backsaw, cut each shoulder to depth.

STEP 14 | Rough in the tenon cheeks with that same backsaw.

STEP 15 | Pare the cheeks down to the line.

STEP 16 | In order for the tenon shoulders — which are cut 90° from the surface of the leg — to mate up tightly with the round pedestal, the top edges of the mortises must be beveled slightly with a paring chisel. Proceed cautiously, testing the leg tenon in the mortise many times as you go.

STEP 17 | You can make a compass for drawing large circles with a nail, a pencil and bit of scrap used as a beam.

STEP 18 | Working on the bottom side of the tabletop panel, place the point of the nail in a shallow drill hole at the panel's center point. Then rotate the compass beam around that center point.

STEP 19 | Use your router to cut a small radius on the top and bottom edges of the tabletop. Then finish the radius with a rasp and sandpaper.

STEP 20 | The tenon at the top of the pedestal fits into a disc that is screwed to the bottom of the tabletop. The radius on the bottom edge of that disc is too large to form with a router; however, you can create that radius on your lathe. Begin by fastening the disc to a face plate with four screws.

STEP 21 | Screw the face plate onto your lathe's drive center.

STEP 22 | It's important that you begin each pass of the fingernail gouge on the edge of the disc closest to you and work away from the disc's center point, toward the edge of the disc closest to the lathe's drive center. If you work the other way, you'll be working uphill against the grain. This inevitably results in significant tear-out. Notice that even though I'm working downhill, I'm still seeing some end-grain tear-out.

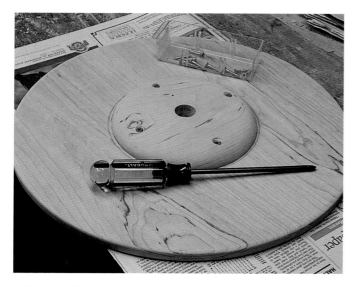

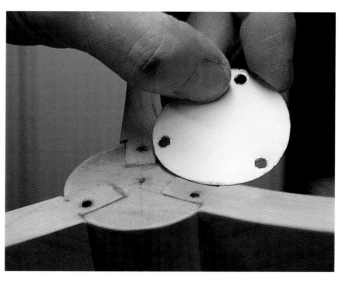

STEP 23 | Fasten the disc to the bottom of the tabletop with four wood screws. Choose a screw length that will allow the screws to penetrate almost completely through the top when the screw head is recessed in the disc. Notice the pitch streaks. This is a common defect in cherry, but it can be placed, as I did here, on hidden surfaces.

STEP 24 | The Shakers screwed a small disc of metal to the bottoms of the legs to help hold them together. On the Shaker originals, the metal disc had three legs, extending out 1" or 2" along the bottom of each leg. I opted for a simpler form, shown here, which still gives me enough reach along each leg to secure it.

STEP 25 | The top side of the tabletop is free of the defects marring the bottom side, visible in step 23.

STEP 26 | Although delicate, this sprightly table should provide years of service in your home.

hanging cupboard

The design of this hanging cupboard makes no allowances for wood shrinkage in either the cabinet back or the door, and each of these panels is large enough to shrink appreciably. With the first incarnation of this particular cupboard, after it had been in our home during a couple of cold winter months, exposed to dry, forced-air heating, I was horrified — but not really surprised — to see that the gap on the unhinged side of the door was three times what it had been when I initially built the piece. The back, too, had shrunk, losing almost $\frac{1}{16}$" on either side. Then, after I got the cupboard into the shop for repair, I saw that the door, which is unconfined in the original design, had begun to cup.

These three problems were all a direct result of two causes. First, the design is inherently flawed. A frame and panel back

and door, like the door on the clock in the next chapter, would have been a much better choice because the central panel floats within its frame, free to expand or contract in response to seasonal fluctuations in relative humidity. Second, I had not done all that I should have done to ensure that my material was as dry as possible. The poplar from which it is built was taken directly into the shop from my unheated wood room. I should, instead, have taken the material into our heated, dry house and stickered it there for several winter months before I began work on this piece.

My solution to the problems posed by this flawed cabinet? I did three things. First, I added a strip to the door's width and refit the panel. Second, I added a narrow strip to each side of the back and refit that panel. Third, I added two cleats to the back of the door to minimize its tendency to cup.

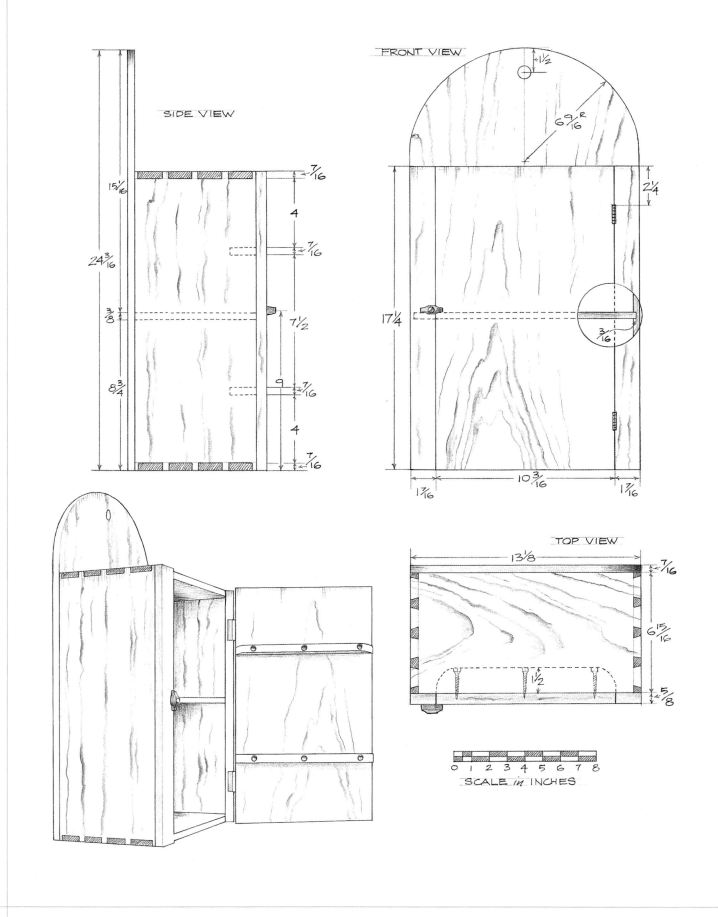

SIDE VIEW

FRONT VIEW

TOP VIEW

SCALE in INCHES

inches (millimeters)

QUANTITY	PART	STOCK	THICKNESS	(mm)	WIDTH	(mm)	LENGTH	(mm)	COMMENTS
1	top	poplar	$7/16$	(11)	$6^{15}/16$	(176)	$13^1/8$	(333)	
2	sides	poplar	$7/16$	(11)	$6^{15}/16$	(176)	$17^1/4$	(438)	
1	bottom	poplar	$7/16$	(11)	$6^{15}/16$	(176)	$13^1/8$	(333)	
1	back	poplar	$7/16$	(11)	$13^1/8$	(333)	$24^3/16$	(615)	
2	stiles	poplar	$5/8$	(16)	$1^7/16$	(36)	$17^1/4$	(438)	
1	door	poplar	$7/16$	(11)	$10^3/16$	(259)	$17^1/4$	(438)	
2	door cleats	poplar	$7/16$	(11)	$1^1/2$	(38)	$10^1/8$	(257)	
1	shelf	poplar	$3/8$	(10)	$6^{15}/16$	(176)	$12^5/8$	(321)	
1	knob	poplar	$1/2$	(13)	$1/2$	(13)	$1^1/4$	(32)	Attaches with one No. 6 × 1" (25mm) brass screw.

NOTE: All dovetail pins and tails should be left $1/32$" (1mm) long so that the excess may be planed and sanded flush.

hardware and supplies

- 4d coated nails
- 4d finish nails
- 2 hinges and screws
- 6 screws for door cleats

STEP 1 | After thicknessing the stock, ripping it to width, cutting it to length and cutting the dadoes for the shelf, cut the through-dovetails that hold the four sides of the case together. (This process is illustrated in steps 90 through 97 in project one.) I should note that the thicknesses of the material in my cabinet are slightly different from the thicknesses of the original, which I believe are visually a bit too great for this fairly small piece. In the original, for example, the door was a full $3/4$" thick.

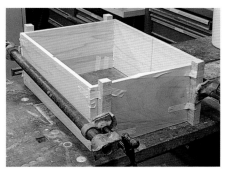

STEP 2 | Bring the four sides of the case together with clamps. Notice the four short strips of scrap under the clamp heads. These do two things: First, they distribute the clamping pressure across the full width of the case sides. Second, they place the clamping pressure behind the pins, allowing them to protrude when the joints are fully seated.

STEP 3 | Check to see that the case is square by measuring the diagonals. If they don't measure the same, rack the longer diagonal against your bench top until they do.

STEP 4 | Cut the back profile on the band saw. Then nail it into place with 4d coated nails driven into predrilled holes. The holes should be a bit smaller than the diameter of the nail.

STEP 5 | Leave the back a bit oversize.

STEP 6 | Then use a block plane to plane it flush with the sides. (If I had waited on this procedure until after the piece had become acclimated to the drier air in my home, I could have avoiding adding material to each side of the box.)

STEP 7 | Tap the shelf into its dadoes, fixing it in place with 4d finish nails. Then, glue the two stiles in place on the front of the cupboard.

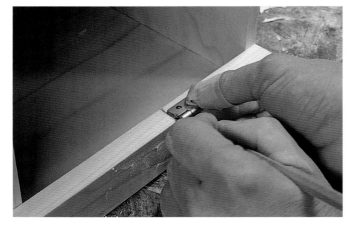

STEP 8 | Mark the hinge locations on the doorjamb.

STEP 9 | Holding your knife against the blade of a try square, score the cross-grained limits of the hinge. Use a short straight-edge to guide the knife when scoring the line along the back side of the hinge.

STEP 10 | With a paring chisel, loosen the waste in the mortise. Then pare back across the grain to remove this waste.

STEP 11 | Pare the mortise to its final depth.

STEP 12 | Place the hinge in its mortise. Then mark the screw holes with a center punch.

STEP 13 | Drill the screw holes in the indentations made by the center punch.

STEP 14 | Hold the door in the correct position. Mark the locations of the hinge mortises on the edge of the door. Cut those mortises just as you cut the mortises in the jamb.

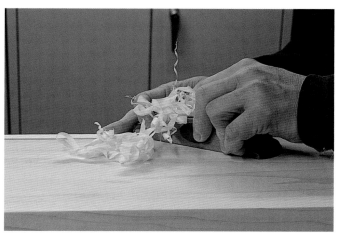

STEP 15 | This photo — taken two months later than ones above — shows the strip I glued to one side of the back to compensate for its shrinkage. After the glue dried, I planed the strip flush with the adjacent cabinet side.

wall clock

This clock is loosely based on a measured drawing by Enjer Handberg, but, as is typical of Handberg's books, the drawing contains no information about joinery or the interior of the case. However, in John Kassay's *The Book of Shaker Furniture*, I found a drawing of a similar clock, which was presented with the necessary construction information. Neither source discussed the interior of the clock, probably because, at least in Kassay's case, the interior layout was dictated by the dimensions of the original clock's wooden movement, a feature few contemporary makers would attempt to reproduce.

After studying the drawings for a week or so, I ordered a battery-driven electrical movement and a face. I then sat down with the movement and the face and sketched a design that, I believe, remains faithful to the look of the original while at the same time accommodates a modern electrical movement.

The movement and face can be purchased from Woodcraft.

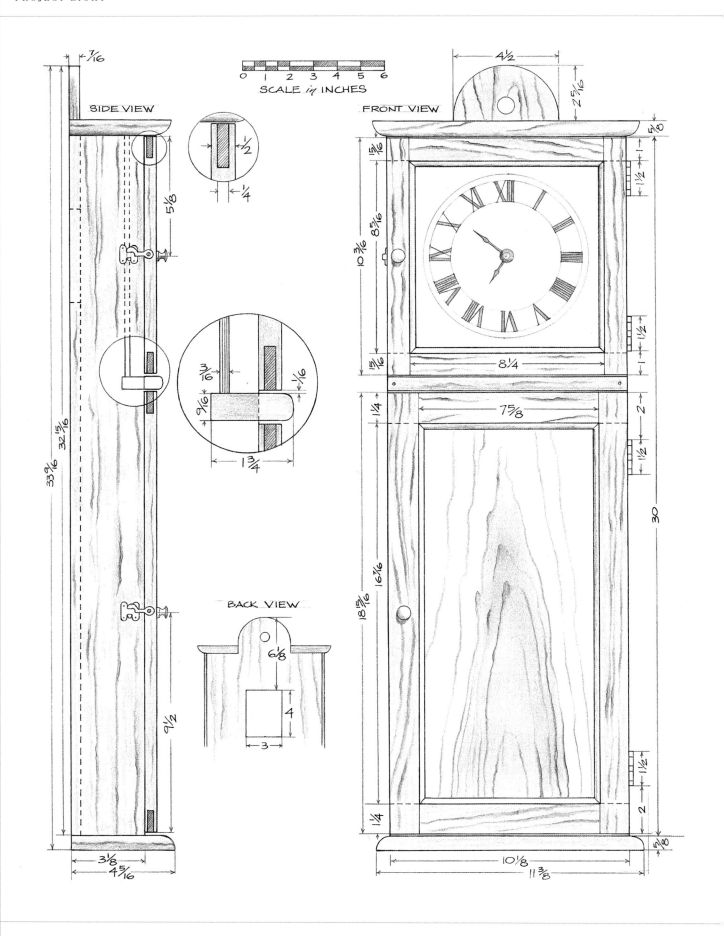

SIDE VIEW

FRONT VIEW

BACK VIEW

SCALE in INCHES

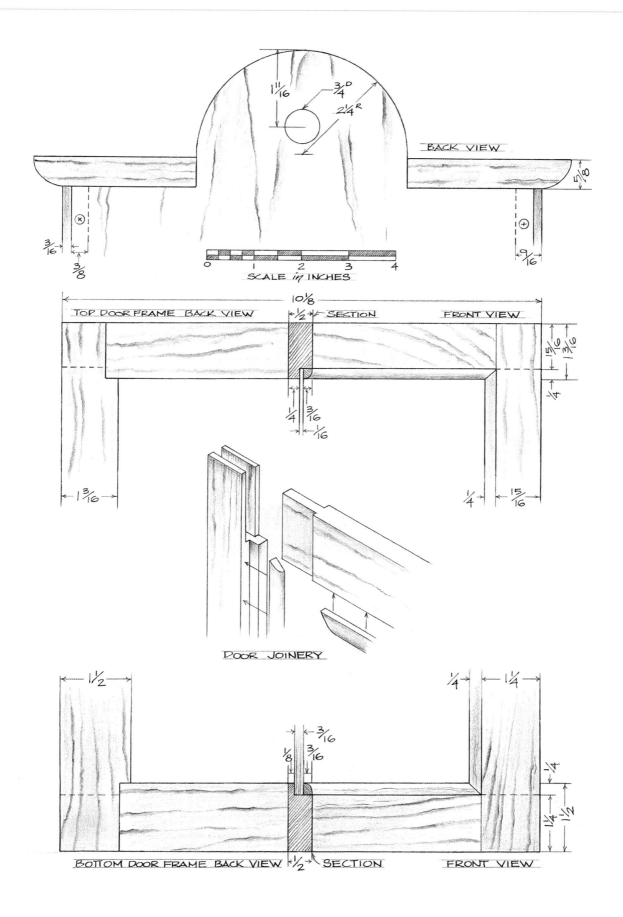

$1\frac{11}{16}$

$\frac{3}{4}^{D}$

$2\frac{1}{4}^{R}$

BACK VIEW

$\frac{5}{8}$

$\frac{3}{16}$

$\frac{3}{8}$

$\frac{9}{16}$

0   1   2   3   4

SCALE in INCHES

$10\frac{1}{8}$

TOP DOOR FRAME BACK VIEW $\frac{1}{2}$ SECTION   FRONT VIEW

$\frac{15}{16}$ $\frac{13}{16}$

$\frac{1}{4}$

$\frac{1}{4}$ $\frac{3}{16}$ $\frac{1}{16}$

$1\frac{3}{16}$

$\frac{1}{4}$ $\frac{15}{16}$

DOOR JOINERY

$1\frac{1}{2}$ $\frac{1}{4}$ $1\frac{1}{4}$

$\frac{3}{16}$ $\frac{3}{16}$ $\frac{1}{8}$

$\frac{1}{4}$

$1\frac{1}{4}$ $\frac{1}{2}$

BOTTOM DOOR FRAME BACK VIEW $\frac{1}{2}$ SECTION   FRONT VIEW

inches (millimeters)

QUANTITY	PART	STOCK	THICKNESS	(mm)	WIDTH	(mm)	LENGTH	(mm)	COMMENTS
2	top & bottom	cherry	$5/8$	(16)	$4^5/_{16}$	(110)	$11^3/_8$	(289)	
2	sides	cherry	$9/_{16}$	(14)	$3^1/_8$	(79)	30	(762)	
1	back	cherry	$7/_{16}$	(11)	$8^{21}/_{32}$	(220)	$32^{15}/_{16}$	(837)	
1	division rail	cherry	$9/_{16}$	(14)	$1^3/_4$	(45)	$10^1/_8$	(257)	
1	piece of glass	cherry	$1/_{16}$	(2)	$8^5/_{16}$ H	(211)	$8^1/_4$ W	(209)	
1	clock face backer	cherry	$1/_4$	(6)	$10^1/_4$	(260)	9	(229)	I fastened the clock face to the clock face backer with two small patches of contact cement.
2	backer cleats	cherry	$3/_4$	(19)	$3/_4$	(19)	$10^1/_4$	(260)	
2	top door rails	cherry	$1/_2$	(13)	$1^3/_{16}$	(30)	$10^1/_8$	(257)	
2	top door stiles	cherry	$1/_2$	(13)	$1^3/_{16}$	(30)	$10^3/_{16}$	(259)	
2	top door short mouldings	cherry	$3/_{16}$	(5)	$1/_4$	(6)	$8^3/_{16}$	(208)	
2	top door long mouldings	cherry	$3/_{16}$	(5)	$1/_4$	(6)	$8^1/_4$	(209)	
2	bottom door rails	cherry	$1/_2$	(13)	$1^1/_2$	(38)	$10^1/_8$	(257)	
2	bottom door stiles	cherry	$1/_2$	(13)	$1^1/_2$	(38)	$18^{15}/_{16}$	(481)	
2	bottom door short mouldings	cherry	$3/_{16}$	(5)	$1/_4$	(6)	$7^9/_{16}$	(192)	
2	bottom door long mouldings	cherry	$3/_{16}$	(5)	$1/_4$	(6)	$16^3/_8$	(416)	
1	bottom door panel	cherry	$1/_4$	(6)	$7^5/_8$	(194)	$16^7/_{16}$	(417)	

hardware and supplies

	Screws
	4d finish nails
2	L-brackets
4	screws
	Glue
	Clockworks and clock face
	Wood screws
	$1/_2$" (13mm) brads
	Hinges, pulls and latches

STEP 1 | Begin by rabbeting the cabinet sides for the installation of the back. (The table saw guard has been removed for the purposes of this illustration. Never operate a table saw without a guard.)

STEP 2 | Screw a backer cleat to the inside surface of each cabinet side. These cleats will give you something against which you can fasten the clock face backer board.

STEP 3 | The division rail that separates the upper and lower doors has a rounded front edge. This could be made with a router, but it's so much easier to rough it in with a few strokes of a block plane. Create the facets at each end with a paring chisel.

STEP 4 | The division rail is held in place primarily by the two brass L-brackets shown in the next two photos; however, before I could install those L-brackets I had to somehow fix the division rail into place. For that purpose I chose a couple of 4d finish nails.

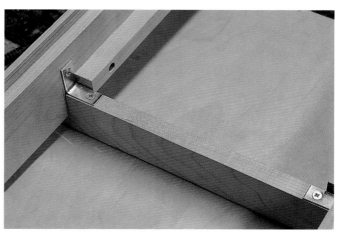

STEP 5 | Mark the locations for the screw holes on the back of the division rail and on the inside surfaces of the cabinet sides. (It's hard to use the center punch here because the case hasn't yet been fastened together securely.)

STEP 6 | Drill the screw holes and install the L-brackets.

STEP 7 | Glue up the back and cut it to the correct shape. Then cut out an access port for the clockworks. The port should be large enough to allow you to get both your hand and the works into position. (You can see the port in step 9.) The original clock had an access port, covered with glass, cut into the side of the cabinet. I would have included it here, but unlike the port on the original clock, which provided a view of the intricately made wooden movements, a glass port on the side of this clock would reveal only the plastic body of the modern clock movement.

STEP 8 | Fasten the back into place with wood screws. The veneer strips are used to evenly distribute the gap on either side of the back panel. A slight gap is necessary to allow for a little wood movement in the back panel.

STEP 9 | This photo shows how the top, back and sides come together.

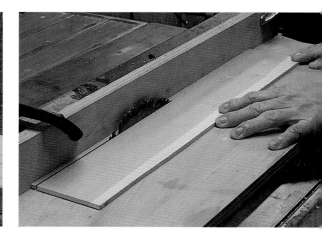

STEP 10 | The original clock — at least, the one drawn by John Kassay — featured doors held together with mortise-and-tenon joinery. However, because they offer more glue surface, I opted for bridle joints. The tenon half of the joint (seen on the part immediately behind my hand) is rough-cut on the table saw with a stack of dado cutters. (This process is demonstrated in steps 33 through 35 in project one.) The mortise for the tenon is cut by hand. Carefully mark the mortise. Define each side with a backsaw. Then run a drill bit through the bottom of the mortise and chip out the waste as shown here.

STEP 11 | Carefully pare the mortise and tenon until they fit together snugly.

STEP 12 | The mouldings that hold the upper-door glass panel and the lower-door wood panel are quite small, so they require some special handling. After thicknessing your moulding stock, rip it into narrow strips as shown here. The wood table and fence, which is screwed together and clamped to the saw fence, allow you to eliminate gaps on either side of the saw blade. This means that the narrow strips won't get caught in the saw throat as you're ripping them out. To use this wood table and fence, you must first lower the saw blade below table height. Then clamp the screwed-together assembly to the saw's metal fence, and slide the saw's metal fence into the correct position and fix it in place. Finally, with the saw running, raise the blade so that it passes through the wood table, and you will have created a gapless throat for your table saw. (The table saw guard has been removed for the purposes of this illustration. Never operate a table saw without a guard.)

STEP 13 | Run the strips through your planer to remove saw marks and to make each one a consistent ³⁄₁₆" square.

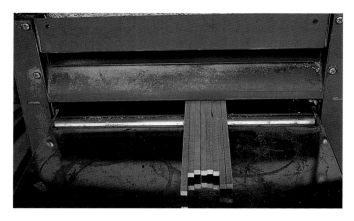

STEP 14 | With a small-radius router bit, create your quarter-round. Notice the featherboard, which allows you to keep the tiny stock pressed against the cutter without endangering your fingers. (The cutter guard was removed for the purpose of this illustration. Never use a router without a guard.)

STEP 15 | With a miter saw, cut the moulding to length and fasten it in place with ¹⁄₂" brads driven through predrilled holes.

STEP 16 | Mount the hinges, pulls and latches. (The hinge-mounting process is described in steps 8 through 14 of project seven.)

STEP 17 | I spent several hours sifting through my lumber piles looking for a piece of cherry displaying the combination of heartwood and sapwood visible in the door panel.

STEP 18 | After I had finished the clock, I discovered that the upper door didn't hang quite right, so I returned the clock to the shop, removed the door and plugged the offending screw holes with wood plugs whittled from a piece of scrap. The plugs were cut to length, glued in place and pared flat. I then drilled new holes.

peg rail

The hanging cupboard in project seven and the wall clock in project eight require a peg rail fitted with unusually small pegs, pegs with a greatest diameter of less than the ³⁄₄" holes at the top of the cupboard and the clock, to hang.

This particular rail and peg set are patterned after examples in John Kassay's *The Book of Shaker Furniture*.

The rail is made by rounding over one edge, as shown in step 78 of project one.

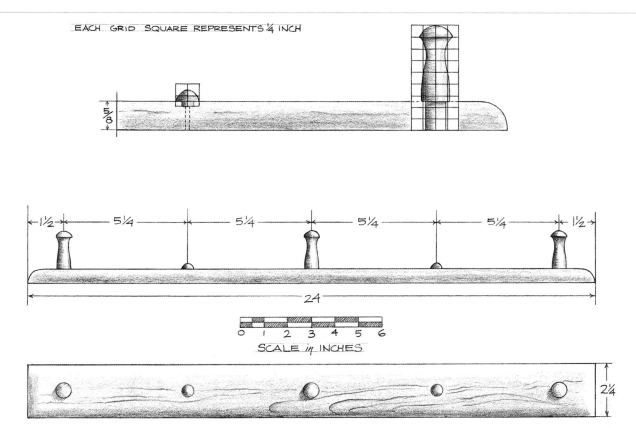

EACH GRID SQUARE REPRESENTS ¼ INCH

SCALE in INCHES

inches (millimeters)

QUANTITY	PART	STOCK	THICKNESS	(mm)	WIDTH	(mm)	LENGTH	(mm)	COMMENTS
3	pegs	cherry	¹¹/₁₆ dia.	(18)			2¼	(57)	
1	rail	cherry	⁵/₈	(16)	2¼	(57)	24	(610)	
2	buttons	cherry	³/₈	(10)	½ dia.	(13)			

NOTE: In my area the cherry ovalhead buttons that conceal the heads of the mounting screws can be purchased locally at Lowe's. They can also be purchased from Woodworker's Supply. Supplier information is located at the end of the book.

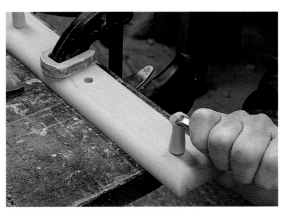

STEP 1 | My original intention was to turn all three pegs from the same length of cherry. However, since the material was so thin I decided to turn two from one length and the third from another. The peg on the right is finished, except for sanding. The peg on the left is ready to be shaped with a ³/₈" fingernail gouge. The process for turning these pegs is the same as that used to turn the knobs for the sewing desk in project one. That process is demonstrated in steps 114 through 116 of project one.

STEP 2 | The easiest way to pare the waste from the end of each peg is to mount it in the rail, which is then clamped to your bench.

10

clothes hangers

If you have a few scraps and a couple of hours' time, you can make a batch of these elegant clothes hangers.

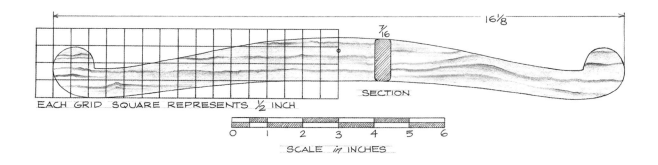

EACH GRID SQUARE REPRESENTS ½ INCH

7/16

SECTION

16⅛

0 1 2 3 4 5 6

SCALE *in* INCHES

inches (millimeters)

QUANTITY	PART	STOCK	THICKNESS	(mm)	WIDTH	(mm)	LENGTH	(mm)	COMMENTS
1	hanger	cherry	7/16	(11)	1 7/16	(36)	16⅛	(409)	

STEP 1 | The relief cuts sawn around the circumference of the hanger's rounded end will allow you to turn this tight circle with a ¼" blade.

STEP 2 | If you have a spokeshave you've never used, here's your opportunity. The inside curves on this hanger can't be reached with a plane, but they can be reached with a spokeshave. If you don't have a spokeshave, a rasp will work quite nicely.

SUPPLIERS

B&Q
B&Q Head Office
Portswood House
1 Hampshire Corporate Park
Chandlers Ford
Eastleigh
Hampshire
SO53 3YX
0870 0101 006
www.diy.com
Tools, paint, wood, electrical, garden

BRIMARC ASSOCIATES
7/9 Ladbroke Park
Millers Road
Warwick
CV34 5AE
0845 330 9100
www.brimarc.com
Woodworking tools and accessories

THE CANING SHOP
926 Gilman Street
Berkeley, California 94710
800-544-3373
www.caning.com
Shaker tape and caning supplies

**CONNECTICUT CANE AND REED
COMPANY**
P.O. Box 762
Manchester, Connecticut 06045
800-227-8498
www.caneandreed.com
Tools, woods, veneers, hardware

CONSTANTINES WOOD CENTER
1040 East Oakland Park Boulevard
Fort Lauderdale, Florida 33334
800-443-9667
www.constantines.com
Cane and reed materials

FOCUS (DIY) LIMITED
Gawsworth House
Westmere Drive
Crewe
Cheshire
CW1 6XB
0800 436 436
www.focusdiy.co.uk
Tools and home woodworking equipment

HOMEBASE LTD
Beddington House
Wallington
Surrey
SM6 OHB
0208 784 7200
www.homebase.co.uk
Tools and home woodworking equipment

THE HOME DEPOT
2455 Paces Ferry Road
Atlanta, Georgia 30339
800-553-3199 (U.S.)
800-668-2266 (Canada)
www.homedepot.com
Tools, paint, wood, electrical, garden

LEE VALLEY TOOLS LTD.
U.S.:
P.O. Box 1780
Ogdensburg, New York 13669-6780
800-267-8735
Canada:
P.O. Box 6295, Station J
Ottawa, Ontario, Canada K2A 1T4
800-267-8761
www.leevalley.com
Bench dogs and other bench hardware

**LOWE'S HOME IMPROVEMENT
WAREHOUSE**
P.O. Box 1111
North Wilkesboro, North Carolina 28656
800-445-6937
www.lowes.com
Tools, paint, wood, electrical,garden

TOOL STATION
18 Whiteladies Road
Clifton
Bristol
BS8 2LG
0808 100 7-2-11
www.toolstation.com
Power tools

WICKES
Wickes House
120-138 Station Road
Harrow
Middlesex
HA1 2QB
0870 6089001
www.wickes.co.uk
Tools and home woodworking equipment

WOODCRAFT
P.O. Box 1686
Parkersburg, West Virginia 26102-1686
800-225-1153
www.woodcraft.com
Woodworking hardware and accessories

WOODWORKER'S SUPPLY
1108 North Glenn Road
Casper, Wyoming 82601
800-645-9292
www.woodworker.com
*Woodworking tools and accessories; finishing
supplies; books and plans*

INDEX

B
Bentwood Boxes and Carriers, 86-97
Boxes and Carriers, Bentwood, 86-97

C
Chairs
    Rocker, Transitional, 80-85
    Rocker, Union Village, 70-79
    Side Chair, Mount Lebanon, 48-69
Clock, Wall, 114-121
Clothes Hangers, 124-125
Cupboard, Hanging, 108-113
Cutting and materials lists
    Bentwood Boxes and Carriers, 88-92
    Clothes Hangers, 125
    Front Rung Mortise Jig, 53
    Hanging Cupboard, 110-111
    Mount Lebanon Side Chair, 50-54
    Peg Rail, 123
    Sewing Desk, 16-19
    Side Rung Mortise Jig, 51-54
    Transitional Rocker, 82-83
    Tripod Table, 100-101
    Union Village Rocker, 72-73
    Wall Clock, 116-118

D
Desk, Sewing, 14-47

F
Front Rung Mortise Jig, 53

H
Hanging Cupboard, 108-113

I
Introduction, 6-12

J
Jigs
    Front Rung Mortise Jig, 53
    Side Rung Mortise Jig, 51-54

M
Mount Lebanon Side Chair, 48-69

P
Peg Rail, 122-123
Projects
    Bentwood Boxes and Carriers, 86-97
    Clothes Hangers, 124-125
    Hanging Cupboard, 108-113
    Mount Lebanon Side Chair, 48-69
    Peg Rail, 122-123
    Sewing Desk, 14-47
    Transitional Rocker, 80-85
    Tripod Table, 98-107
    Union Village Rocker, 70-79
    Wall Clock, 114-121

R
Rocker, Transitional, 80-85
Rocker, Union Village, 70-79

S
Seat weaving, 68-69
Sewing Desk, 14-47
Side Chair, Mount Lebanon, 48-69
Side Rung Mortise Jig, 51-54
Suppliers, 126

T
Table, Tripod, 98-107
Transitional Rocker, 80-85
Tripod Table, 98-107

U
Union Village Rocker, 70-79

W
Wall Clock, 114-121
Weaving, seat, 68-69

The best woodworking projects come from Popular Woodworking Books!

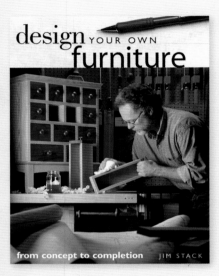
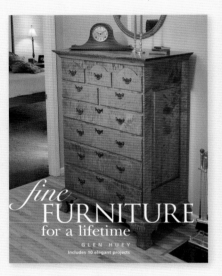
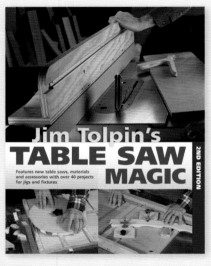